The Cash Machine

The Cash Machine

Using the Theory of Constraints for Sales Management

A Business Novel

By Richard Klapholz and Alex Klarman

The North River Press Publishing Corporation

Additional copies of this book can be obtained from your local
bookstore or the publisher:

The North River Press Publishing Corporation
P.O. Box 567
Great Barrington, MA 01230
(800) 486-2665 or (413) 528-0034

www.northriverpress.com

Manufactured in the United States of America

ISBN: 0-88427-177-3

Table of Contents

Chapter 1
The Hot Seat

October 20, Year 1

Gary is going to drop the bomb in a few minutes. We are all gathered in the management conference room with Gary, our boss, and all the VP's of Carmen Graphic Solutions. I see the faces of John, Tim, Eliza, Ron and Pierce. They don't smile. The meeting was arranged so quickly. Much too quickly for it to be an opportunity to share some good news.

All our top management is here. John is our production chief. Tall, dark and not very handsome, he is the idol of our manufacturing guys. He has risen through the ranks starting as foreman seven years ago, to VP of Production. He took his engineering classes in the evenings, never missing a day of work. Tim, a slim and smiling guy, is CGS's secret weapon to all customers' complaints. I don't know how he does it, but after a short chat with Tim, even the angriest customers start seeing our side, too. It's no wonder that in the course of two short years, he has climbed the organizational ladder from being a field representative in the Midwest to being our VP of Customer Support.

Eliza, a top graduate in Economics from Princeton, has been serving as CFO for the last nine years. Today, she is also our CIO. Sharp, honest and outspoken, she is highly revered even by the cynical crowd of Wall Street analysts. Ron – well, by now everybody knows Ron. He was a member of the mythological team, which developed our Model 100 close to twenty-five years ago. Model 100 was our first product and also the first digital editing station commercially available on the market. It has forever changed the way complex printing jobs are executed. It was Model 100 that put our company, CGS, firmly in the marketplace. Today Ron leads our R&D group, which we all still refer to as Engineering.

Pierce, well, Pierce is our VP of Sales. At this point, he's the only one who knows what's going to happen next. I don't dare to look at him – at least for now. He avoids my eyes, too.

"While we have made major improvements in engineering and production, our sales have stopped growing in the last three quarters." Gary, our President & CEO, is more determined than ever. "Our sales have grown, on average, by twenty percent or better each year for seven years now. Pierce has been part of that growth throughout all that period, first as our East Region Sales Manager, and in the last two years as our VP of Sales. We are all very grateful to you Pierce." Pierce puts his salesman smile on his face. I continue avoiding his eyes.

Gary continues with a firm tone: "The pressure from our board is becoming unbearable, especially since we are losing market share. At this pace, we will have to start taking drastic actions, including painful cost-cutting measures, within two quarters. I have served with Carmen Graphic Solutions for over twenty years now. I know most of our employees personally. I intend to avoid layoffs at all cost." Gary has been a successful CEO for more than five years now. I know he's planning to retire in a year or two. He must hate the thought of ending his career at CGS in such a way, and perhaps even with layoffs. The guy probably doesn't sleep at night.

He continues: "In the last few days, I have given a lot of thought to our situation. Our core customers buy less, in spite of the fact that the market for our products is expanding. We simply are not there to take advantage of that fact. A change in our approach is needed. I am hereby announcing a change in the executive management of CGS. As of Monday next week, Pierce will move from Sales to Marketing, and Roger will take responsibility for Sales. I have talked to both of them this morning and I am happy to say that both Pierce and Roger have agreed to take on their new challenging assignments."

"Gary," Eliza is first to react, "Pierce knows all our customers intimately. If I am not mistaken, he has himself, directly and indirectly, generated over half a billion dollars in sales for CGS. Roger, with no offense to you – you know that you have all my respect – you have not been in Sales since you joined CGS. Gary, are we sure this is the right time to change horses? Excuse my expression."

Eliza, our CFO, is as sharp and direct as always. She brings me back to my morning discussion with Gary. Gary asked Amy, his assistant, to have me join him in his office. When I entered, he stood up and closed the door. I immediately knew that something was up. Gary was very direct:

"Roger, I want to move you, instead of Pierce, to Sales. I need your strategic thinking and your creativity. Our market is changing very fast now and we are losing track. To be fair, I don't know what to do anymore. Pierce and I come from the same school; we have both been selling for a long time. Maybe too long. You know that we have been implementing the solutions based upon the Theory of Constraints (TOC) in Production and in Engineering with great success. I've asked Barry, our TOC consultant, to also try and work with Pierce, but you know Pierce, he is so self-confident that he thinks that his approach to sales is the only right one. He believes that the current slow-down in sales is just a temporary phenomenon. I don't agree with him. But I'm afraid, so it seems, that after all, you can't teach an old dog new tricks."

"Gary, so what are you planning to do with Pierce?" I ask, hesitantly.

"I will swap between the two of you. He'll become our VP of Marketing and Business Development."

"You must be kidding me. Our success depends on our customer relationships. Pierce has it all, and besides, he will never forgive me."

"There's nothing to be forgiven. It is my decision, not yours. Roger, I am asking for your support. I have thought about it a lot. Will you take on this challenge?" What can one say in such a situation?

"Sure, Gary." I just hope my voice doesn't betray what I really feel. "You have my full support!"

As usual, I put myself in impossible situations. Joanna always tells me that I make decisions too fast. But I guess I'm too old to change now. So here I am – jumping from the comfortable chair of marketing to the high-pressure, fast-changing, quarterly-driven stool of Sales. Yes, ladies and gentlemen, I am Roger Mirton, Vice President of Sales for Carmen Graphics Solutions. Who would have believed this just a week ago? By the way, what's this TOC thing and what the hell does Theory of Constraints have to do with sales? I have no clue. It's just a manufacturing thing, isn't it? There is so much going through my head right now.

Gary interrupts my thoughts. "Roger, are you with us?"

"I'm sorry, Gary. Yes, you have my full attention."

"I was just responding to Eliza about how we will continue to rely on Pierce in terms of getting the most out of his relationships with customers. However, let there be no doubts, Roger is now in charge. I am sure that you will all support him fully."

"Yes, we will."

Well, unanimous it wasn't. But it's good to know that at least John and Tim are on my side. Pierce remains quiet. Very quiet. That's not like him. And Ron, our VP of Engineering, is quiet too. I definitely prefer the gutsy comments from Eliza to their silence. I will need to rely heavily on the backing of Gary, and whatever assistance I can muster from John, Tim and Eliza. With Ron and Pierce, I have the uneasy feeling; it's a totally different story

*　　*　　*

Carmen Graphics Solutions is a leader in imaging and software technology. We supply equipment to all segments of the graphic arts industry. Ray Samuel founded the company over twenty-five years ago. Ray is now the Chairman of the Board of CGS, and is no longer active in the day-to-day operations. Ray owns 10 percent of the company personally, other shareholders own around 20 percent and the rest is public on the NASDAQ. I still remember the party that was thrown for all company employees in North America when Ray announced that CGS had crossed half a billion dollars in annual sales. He announced his early retirement and the appointment of Gary Calleso to the position of President & CEO. Gary was VP of Sales prior to that. He is a clever guy and I enjoy working for him and with him. Under Gary, CGS has continued to grow to a revenue level of 750 million dollars per year. But recently, something has happened. We've had three consecutive quarters of decline and we are now back at below 700 million. The share price has taken a big hit and has fallen from $45 to $18. Ray and the Board are putting a lot of pressure on Gary. This is perhaps the most challenging time of his whole career. And now, he has put me in the middle of it all.

*　　*　　*

It has been a long and tough day so I decide to head home early. It's been snowing all day in Bedford, Massachusetts, and it's freezing outside. I need to wipe the snow from the windshield. It takes me about fifty minutes to get home. This is twenty-five minutes longer than it usually takes me. When I arrive, Joanna is already at home. Jennifer is probably in her room; she's fifteen now and she lives in a world of her own. Lizzie is in the kitchen with Joanna. Lizzie turned twelve this year. Now that I'm here, the whole Mirton family is safe at home, just me and my three beautiful ladies!

"Hi, Jo. How was your day today?"

"Great. How was yours? Did Gary announce your new appointment?"

"He did. I think everyone is still a little shocked. Some are willing to give it a chance but others believe that Gary's going crazy. The fact remains that our shares have fallen sharply and we need to do something about it."

One of these so-called analysts had the nerve to call it a *"musical chairs game,"* while other said that *"if CGS' management thinks that a better arrangement of chairs on the deck can save this **Titanic** from sinking, then they better think again."*

"Does this mean no more options money? You were talking about a few hundred thousand at the next vesting time, hadn't you?"

"Yeah! The exercise price is nineteen dollars and the share is now at eighteen dollars. We can forget about selling for quite a while and, if I screw up my new promotion, we can forget about it forever. The stakes are very high here."

"Dad, does it mean that now we are going to be poor people?" Lizzie has her own interpretation for our discussion. She also has the tendency to participate in our conversations, even when she's not invited to do so. As a matter of fact, especially when she isn't.

"No, Lizzie. It simply means that moving to a new house is no longer part of our plans for the next year or so."

"That's cool. I like where we are anyway. I hate the thought of being far away from my friends." At least someone is happy that we potentially lost close to half a million dollars recently.

"Jo, it's almost solely up to me now to increase sales. Believe me, the pressure will be huge. Also, I'll have to travel big time. I truly don't know where to start!"

"Roger, calm down. I know you can make it. Just approach this the same way you always approach difficult situations – and you'll succeed. Think. Think, think, and think again. You have our support. You can trust Jennifer, Lizzie and me. Right Lizzie?"

"Yes, Daddy, you are the best."

"Thanks, my dear ones."

We're now closing the year. I guess that Ray, our Chairman, and Gary have given up on this year. They want me to deliver results starting from Q1 next year. This leaves us something like 30-40 days to start the turnaround. But CGS is a lot different from when I started working here; it's a large company now. To make a significant change won't be easy. The best thing I can do for now is to have a glass of wine and go to sleep. As Scarlett O'Hara has said, tomorrow is another day.

The snow really changes the landscape completely in New England. What used to be a barren area, strewn with leafless trees, is now a magical, white landscape. They said on the news that a cold front is on its way and there would be a snowstorm by the end of the week. But at work everything boils.

After a few days of getting into the job and talking with the regional sales managers, I am attempting to get some control of the end-of-year quarter. The level of uncertainty is very high. Most orders will come, if they come, within the last days of the quarter. Which also happen to be the last days of the year. This means that on the top of the usual end-of the-quarter fight for additional orders we have the end-of-the-year struggle for better P&L results. The pressure is huge and is becoming unbearable. I spend nearly all the first part of the week on the short-term items, realizing that if the short-term is representative of Q1 that starts in a few weeks from now, I am in deep trouble.

The morning drive is the best time for thoughts – at least for me. In the morning, I'm still sharp in my thinking and not bothered by the events of the day. I often turn to 102.5 FM and listen to classical music. Sometimes, like now, I simply shut the radio off to think. I need to re-analyze the situation. Let's start from the beginning. We have good products. We have a healthy, growing market. We have assembled the best possible people. The management team is improvement-driven and, relatively speaking, non-political, except maybe for Pierce. Still, our sales are going down and we're losing market share. If I want to succeed, I need to have an almost immediate impact on the business.

The problem is definitely a sales problem. Isn't it? I don't really know. Let's put that aside for a while. Let's assume it is a pure sales problem. How does one resolve a sales dip? All the standard solutions come to mind: replace all the sales guys, invest heavily in marketing promotions, train our sales guys better, increase our sales support staff, focus our sales guys on a smaller amount of products and solutions, have our service guys sell products too. I'm shooting into thin air – I know it – and I hate it. This is not systematic at all. I know one thing: I can't rely on luck because luck has nothing to do with it. Intuition doesn't do it anymore either. There is another tempting move: quit before it is too late. I feel like I'm really starting to panic now. I need to put some order in my thoughts. What did Joanna say? Think, think, and think again.

Let's think about what Pierce did just a year ago. Yes, I remember it now. He invested in sales channel expansion. He had realized that the problem lies in insufficient market coverage. He did well. He added more sales guys and recruited a few reps in certain remote geographies. Maybe Gary simply didn't give him enough time. I just need to continue with what he did and be more patient. But who the hell has time for patience. Roger Mirton, I say to myself, you need to bring an improvement in less than 45 days – an improvement that is both visible and real at the same time. The improvement needs to be significant and sustainable. Patience or luck is not the right approach.

So let's try everything at once, let's bring out the heavy artillery, like they say in war movies. Let's replace all sales guys, let's invest heavily in marketing promotion, let's launch an aggressive training program for our new sales guys, let's expand our sales channels even further, let's add another 10 or 15 people to our sales support staff, let's focus on a smaller amount of products and solutions, and so on and so forth. Sure, and Eliza, our tough-as-nails CFO, will happily allocate the budgets. This will all happen at once. Gosh, it's only eight in the morning and I'm already hallucinating. I'll need to talk to Gary when I arrive. I call Amy. She is already there. I ask her to set a one-on-one meeting with Gary first thing in the morning. Fortunately, Gary is available and takes the meeting. I am already at Exit 32 on I 95. So I'll be in the office early today.

*   *   *

I have time to quickly skim the first e-mails of the morning, prepare some coffee, and here I am again in Gary's office. I present my case to Gary:

"Pierce has relied greatly on his intuition, and his long-time experience. To be fair, I can't see what he has done wrong. Even more, I would say that he did everything right, and the results are still disappointing."

"Let's go through it together – okay?" I don't think Gary knows what Pierce did wrong either, but he wants to give this a chance with me. So I start my analysis:

"Pierce assumed that he could generate more sales with better coverage of the market. The assumption was that we simply did not have enough feet on the street. The market was buying, and willing to buy more, but we were simply not there to take the orders. There were too many deals closed in which we were not even part of the sales cycle! Pierce knew that his only chance to increase sales was to expand coverage. So he added more sales people and he signed on representative agents all over the country. You remember when he and I presented the case and you approved it, don't you?"

"Yep! You did a great job presenting and… well, selling your case. It made a lot of sense at the time." Gary really wants to help me. I can really feel it. I hope that we'll be able to come to the right conclusions fast! I continue:

"So let's recap. Pierce, with the help of Marketing, did it. And at least for a while it worked. It took us six months to hire the sales guys and the reps and to properly train them. From that point on, we saw two quarters of steady increase in sales. You remember how good we all looked when we presented our results to the Board."

"You bet. We were heroes that day." But both Gary and I also remember what happened next: the steady decrease in sales. I go on:

"Well, this is where I start to lose it! We have good products, the market is buying, our sales channels cover all the market and our people really know how to sell and still…"

"Listen, Roger, you know that we've worked with a consultant on improving our operations for many months now. His name is Barry Kahn. He's a TOC expert and has really helped us a lot. When we last met, I mentioned the problems we were having in sales and he indicated that there wasn't much of a difference between selling and producing!"

"Come on, Gary. You must be kidding. That's what he said? No difference between selling and manufacturing? You know that I could never produce anything, and that John could never sell anything!" Then I immediately remember that one of the reasons why Gary selected me for this position is my openness to new ideas. Well, at least I have to behave as if I am. "Okay, Gary. I'll meet with this Barry. Uhh, I have to run. I can't afford to be late to the weekly ops meeting. See you later."

"Bye, Roger."

I decide to have a look in one of my management books regarding TOC. Well, that's an easy one – except for some trivial remarks, which say nothing, it's hardly mentioned at all. OK, the books are mostly from the mid-eighties, so I decide to look for something more updated; I go on the web. That's easy too. But what's one supposed to do when one and a half million pages of information are at one's disposal? How to find the proverbial needle in such an endless stack of hay? I have a quick look at some of the sites. One arouses my interest; it claims that TOC intends to turn management from an art into science. From an activity which is mainly dependent on the gift of the individual, which is irreproducible, and is almost impossible to transfer to others – into something that's structured, reproducible and ruled by a set of laws and rules one's capable of learning and understanding. And it claims its application is based upon a set of methodologies that are called 'Thinking Processes'. That seems to be exactly what I need if I'm to follow Joanna's advice – think.

Further, it claims that TOC's basic tenet is that all (or most) of the phenomena one encounters in, say, an organization, are interconnected. Not an eclectic collection of independent phenomena, but rather a set of things connected by clear and easily recognizable cause-and-effect relationships.

It's for a reason (or a cause) that particular results were achieved – and we are perfectly capable of understanding such a causal relationship. Which means one can analyze the reality, reach conclusions regarding the causes of a particular phenomenon, say – failure, and then attempt to change the causes of it.

It all makes sense to me; I've always believed that luck alone doesn't bring success, and a lack of it doesn't necessarily lead to failure. I think, according to how I see it, that TOC is rather a common-sense approach to management. Not a computer system and not a religion. At least this is something I can start to comprehend.

And yes, the constraints that are a part of the methodology name (Theory of Constraints) are simply the things that limit (or in worst case - even totally prevent) the system from reaching its goals. You know, like when there is an accident on the highway, two lanes are closed and the entire traffic crawls on the single one still open. The point at which the accident happens is turned into a bottleneck, which, in turn, dictates the rate at which all the traffic moves. The fact that three lanes are open to traffic before and after that point has no importance; it's this single point that dictates the traffic capacity of this particular stretch of the road.

As I understand it, TOC claims that the performance of the entire system is governed by rather a very small set of constraints. If you are capable of identifying them, you can then use them to leverage the entire system. Knowing the identity of the constraints enables one to assess the potential of an entire system without going into too many details. To understand TOC even deeper, I'll leave it to our TOC consultant. That's what we pay him for, isn't it?

*　　　*　　　*

Chapter 2
The Selling Machine

November 15, Year 1

Today we're doing the big splash around the launch of our newest color scanner. This is a high-end system that is aimed at scanning professional photography images for the highest quality ads. It incorporates full automation, which is quite unique in that domain. We call it the Lilly. It is probably the most expensive system of its kind. Certainly, it is the best. We have been under a lot of pressure from our competitors lately. Hopefully, the Lilly will put us back in the game. Although I originally started the planning of the Lilly launch activities, Pierce completely took over. He has added his own style. He and Ron, our VP of Engineering, have really augmented the profile of the launch. They have gathered a full-fledged press conference at the beautiful (and prohibitly expensive) Mt. Washington Hotel in New Hampshire. I'm afraid to ask how much this has cost us during peak holiday time. The guys from the press will have a good time skiing on the beautiful slopes of Breton Woods in the afternoon and perhaps even tomorrow morning. I guess this is a good enough incentive to have them feature the Lilly on the front page of their respective magazines.

Pierce is the star of the conference. He loves it. His speech to the press continues:

"For the demanding needs of today's scanning-intensive graphic businesses, where maximum speed and excellent image quality are essential, the Lilly is the answer. The top-of-the-line scanner from Carmen Graphics Solutions, the Lilly delivers the kind of ultra-high resolution, extended dynamic range and color depth that today's professionals require. With Lilly, unbeatable reliability, extreme sharpness and image detail go hand in hand with speed. Our customers will be able to quickly produce high volumes of scans to meet the tightest deadlines at the highest possible scanning performance."

I'll skip the fireworks, the special effects and the music band. This is the biggest launching event in our history. I must admit that it's a bit too much for my taste, but I decided not to oppose it in the management meetings because I need the support of Pierce and Ron. This is not the time for me to fight against them. When I asked how many Lilly's we have already installed in the field, Pierce looked at me as if I was killing him. So I kept mum. From what I know, the Lilly is still in the labs going through extensive testing. Ron mentioned in the meeting that he was very confident that the Lilly would be ready for deliveries in Q1 next year. Ron has been in engineering for twenty-five years now and probably knows what he's doing. Still, I am a bit nervous about this. I wish I had gotten some feedback from customers about the new system.

*   *   *

I opt not to ski with the journalists. I am back in the office. While Gary, Ron and Pierce are entertaining their guests in the mountains, I have some time to meet with Barry. Serious guy. His thick, black hair is starting to whiten. He looks more like one of our foremen than a management consultant. I decide not to mention my foray into the Internet to find information on TOC and wait to hear about it from the horse's mouth.

"So, Barry, you are our resident TOC guru. I know that you have been very involved with John and Ron. What is TOC anyway?"

"Well, Roger, TOC stands for Theory of Constraints. And although I'm deeply convinced that TOC provides for better management, I don't think I'm a guru. But it's okay if you call me that anyway. I'd be more than happy to present its concepts to you, but if you don't mind – and I can only guess how skeptical you may be at this point – I prefer to ask a few questions first in order to put the concepts in practice immediately. I believe that we can achieve a lot in our first meeting."

"No problem Barry. Go ahead, ask your questions!"

"Okay. Thanks. What led you, or Pierce at the time, to increase sales coverage?"

"That's an easy one. In all territory reviews, we were hearing the same tune: customers were buying without us even knowing that they were in buying mode. We were losing deals because we were not even competing on them. We simply didn't get those deals because we had no one to call on those customers."

"I see. Did you or Pierce divide your selling process in to distinct, well-defined stages?"

"Yes, sure, we have what we call our ten Steps-of-Sale. No wonder everybody calls it SOS," I say, trying to be humorous.

Barry doesn't even smile. He asks: "What are they?"
"Well, that's very simple. I start reciting what I've learned in the last month by heart. The ten steps are:

1. *Selection*: selecting customers that fit our target markets based on well-defined criteria set by Marketing. Not too long ago, I was VP of Marketing, so I basically set those criteria.

2. *Qualification*: this is a set of basic, general questions that we ask the selected customers. This will define if they really are in need of the type of equipment we sell.

3. *Needs Assessment*: here we ask specific questions. We thereby learn which solution to offer to the prospect. As you know, our product portfolio is quite extensive. This is almost always done as an on-site visit by one of our sales guys. A sales-support person sometimes accompanies him or her.

4. *Letter of Understanding*: once we believe we understand the customer's needs, we simply write a letter or e-mail, which verbalizes our understanding of their needs. This is the one stage in the whole sales cycle where correcting mistakes costs the least and is the most effective.

5. *Presentation Demo*: this can happen in many ways; at a show, at a reference account, or at one of our demo centers. We don't typically use the specific customer data for that demo. This is more of a product overview.

6. *Solution Proposal and Technical Check*: our sales and sales support teams prepare together a detailed proposal for the customer.

7. *Production Demo*: here we benchmark specific customer jobs. This very often makes or breaks the deal.

8. *Quotation Submission*: very simple – a price quotation, with a complete description of the solution offered and why it matches the customer needs.

9. *Negotiation*.

10. *Closing*."

"Wow, that's very extensive. Do you use the funnel concept at all?"

"Sure. Barry, I really don't want to offend you, but this is all sales 101. I have been in sales or in marketing for twenty years now."

"Roger, please bear with me. This may seem tedious at first, but we need a systematic approach here. I need you to give me some credit."

"Okay. Sorry! The funnel. Go ahead."

"Just to make sure we use a common language here. The input to the funnel is prospects, but not any prospect – I would only take qualified ones. The output of the funnel is closed deals or customers. One very often talks about the 'hit ratio': how many qualified prospects we were able to turn into closed deals. We also carefully follow the time it has taken from input to output, from having selected our potential clients to a closed deal with them. Obviously, the higher the "hit ratio" and the shorter the time in the funnel, the more efficient our selling 'machine' is."

Barry makes a drawing on a sheet of paper in front of him:

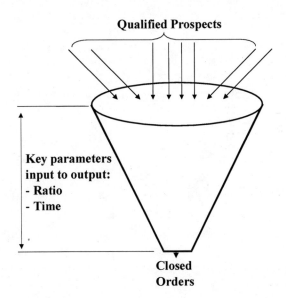

"Now, for the average sales person at CGS, if – say – you'd put twenty-five prospects after the qualification process, which is step-of-sale 2, how many of those do you typically close?"

I think a little while and then come up with an answer.

"I think that on average, about four to five closed deals. Our closing ratio hovers around five or six to one. Some of it is because of our coverage. Although our coverage is much improved, it is still not completely airtight."

"For those that you do close, how long is the average time from step three to step ten."

"Our average sales cycle is around one hundred days. There are some repeat sales that we close in a week. But there are also some cycles that take almost a full year. The average is one hundred days."

"Good. Thanks, Roger. You told me that a while ago you heard about many cases in which you were not even aware that a prospect was in buying mode. I guess that you overcame that to a large extent with better coverage."

"You bet we did. Hey, our sales have increased by over twenty percent since then. You can't even compare."

"Sure, that's great. Now tell me about the problems Sales faces. Try to recall the last sales meetings with your guys. Can you repeat the five most common complaints or concerns of the sales guys?"

"Well, let me think. I made many notes. Give me a few minutes to find them." Usually, I try to write things down but then the problem becomes finding the notes. "Here they are. I haven't had time to reconcile them yet. Let's see. A few guys talked about readiness of some of the new products. More than once complained about overpriced products. Here I have some notes about difficulty to book a production demo. Some more notes about some competitive products from a strong and aggressive Japanese supplier. I guess I could find more if I could get my notes more organized."

"Roger, what are the steps that are sometimes bypassed in the selling cycle and which steps are never bypassed and are absolutely mandatory?"

"Well, Barry, it depends. First and foremost it has to do with if we're talking about a brand new customer, a repeat sale, or a new product to an existing customer. For a new product, we may use all of the steps. For a repeat sale, we may often use only steps eight and ten; quotation submission and closing. We don't utilize steps four and five all of the time—Letter of Understanding and Presentation Demo, which is unfortunate because I see those as quite critical."

"Is there always a Production Demo?"

"Except for repeat sales, I'd say that we have a Production Demo on ninety percent of the cases."

"I see. Well, Roger, you now have some food for thought. What we both understand now is that you have a sequential process that consists of ten steps. The time it takes to get from one step to another is still somewhat unclear, but we have a pretty good idea what the overall time is to complete a cycle. There is some uncertainty in the process. In other words, it might take one day to negotiate a deal with one customer, but it might take five or more days with another one. Nobody really knows. Roger, I have some good news: TOC deals exactly with those type of problems, and provides a systematic way to bring about significant improvements in a short amount of time."

"Barry, as you see, I am definitely willing to give it a chance. What's next?" I hope that I don't sound too desperate. But in a way, I am.

"First, you need to familiarize yourself with what your colleagues John and Ron did with TOC in Production and in Engineering, respectively. I have brought a few books for you to read."

Barry points to a stack of books on the table. The guy must be nuts, if he thinks that I can squeeze a literature class into my crazy schedule. It's not that I don't like reading. I do. A lot. But now? My face must be betraying me, as he hastily adds: "Don't waste time; take a day off if needed. In the mean time, you need to ask some analyst in your IT department to run some data. I heard that CGS has implemented a nice sales tracking system. Can you find out how many prospects are in any step at any given time?"

"Yes, we can. I'm not too familiar with the system yet. I know that Pierce didn't make much use of it while overseeing the entire sales organization. He explained to me that it is more a tool for usage at the district sales management level and below."

"Roger, we will need the data in your system. Can you please get the information for our next meeting?"

"You can count on it."

I still don't know what to think. Barry just left my office and I realized that he never even mentioned what TOC actually is. Not a word. He just said that TOC deals with our type of problems and provides systematic solutions for improvement, and then left four books on my desk. It seems like this guy is a great proponent of self-learning. He wants me to leave the office and read instead of selling. I should keep this quiet. If Ray or Gary or Pierce hears about this, I won't be able to show my face at CGS for the next couple of days.

*   *   *

When I get home that night, I tell Joanna that I need to retire to the den because I have some urgent reading material. When she sees it's a book I'm carrying, and not the standard stack of reports I've been bringing home lately, she is quick to react.

"Are you becoming a student again?"

"In a way, yes. The only issue is that I need to be a quick learner. I don't have a lot of time. But at least we don't have to pay for tuition."

The Cash Machine

"So go on, my dear. Take your time. Who knows… if the books are any good, I may read them, too."

"Sure. We can then even talk about them." And my middle name will be Mr. TOC, I say to myself.

Joanna has worked in education throughout her entire career. Recently, she completed a M.A. in Educational Management. Now, she is a vice-principal in a nearby high school. She deals with teens from around fifteen to eighteen years old. That's a challenging job. Maybe even more challenging than mine. But I really can't see how my books on TOC can be of any help to her! Anyway, I put myself at ease and dive into the books.

*   *   *

It takes me just a few days to read all four books. I must say that, surprisingly, I quite enjoy the process. Here and there, I had to re-read a paragraph or two, but overall, the reading was relatively easy. I think that these new type of books, namely 'business novels,' are an effective way to convey new management methods. Who knows, if I'm successful with the turnaround at CGS, I may write one myself. Gosh, I must be in delirium mode again. I don't even know where to start the turnaround, and I'm already talking about its successful conclusion. This is not optimism. This is foolishness.

Anyway, I somehow make it to the office this morning. I am too deep in my thoughts. I don't even remember if there was heavy traffic or not; I guess I was driving on automatic pilot. When I arrive, I call Chris, Sales' business analyst, to my office. I give him a short spiel about the 10 Steps-of-Sale and about the Theory of Constraints. Well, at least the little I know about it. I ask him to do some analysis for me. He is a quick learner and he grasps what I need in less than half an hour. If I know him, I'll have hard data by the end of the day today.

Luckily, we have that sales tracking system in place. It is part of a complete CRM system, but I don't think that we at CGS implement the real philosophy of Customer Relationships Management across the board. The advantages of our sales tracking are big: first, we now have a history of what we do in Sales. In the past, everything used to be in some personal folders filed somewhere. When a sales guy was leaving, or when we were re-assigning territories, everything had to be redone from the very beginning; we were a company without history. Now, we really hold most of the information; especially contact information and sales quotations. Another big advantage is that we were able to replace all spreadsheets with a centralized database and a nice tool that retrieves all necessary information.

Today, we mostly use it to see where we are in the quarter and to forecast where we might be at the end of the quarter. I mean in dollar terms. Also, we can have a pretty good in-the-quarter forecast for the equipment that we'll need to deliver once we close the orders. This has really helped our order administration and production guys. The system holds much more information than that and I guess that some of it is used at the district management level or even at the individual sales person level. For me, it's basically a tool that lets me know what we have in the pipeline. It is an online aggregate of the individual forecasts. Those individual forecasts are reviewed by the District Sales Managers and then by the Regional Sales Managers. This is done on an ongoing basis. Knowing Chris and his analytical skills, it should be pretty straightforward for him to retrieve the information that Barry and I need to progress in our endeavors.

Barry and I are in my office again. I was right. Chris was able to crunch the numbers by the end of the same day and, after looking at it two days ago, I e-mailed the information to Barry. So, I've done my part and presented the case to him. Barry has obviously done his homework as well. He sounds excited.

"Well, as a physician would say, my diagnosis is as follows: when you started, your constraint was a bottleneck in Step One:

Selection. You did not have enough prospects selected to enter the funnel. You solved that with your additional sales guys and reps. We call the activity of turning a constraint into something that doesn't limit the system anymore a 'constraint (or bottleneck) elevation' in our production terminology. Unfortunately, or perhaps fortunately, this is a never-ending process of continuous improvement. What limits your sales now is clearly a new bottleneck, which is most probably Step Seven: Production Demo. It <u>no longer matters how many sales channels you add, as long you don't squeeze more of your prospects through</u> step <u>seven. I would even say that if you add any more sales prospects it would be a waste of resources and money</u>! Does this make sense?"

I look at the numbers I got from Chris, and carefully answer:

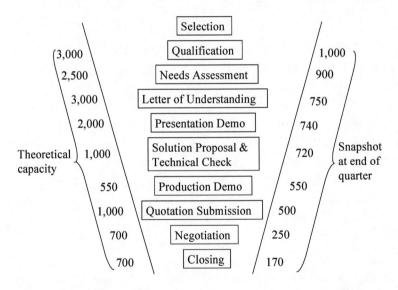

Theoretical capacity			Snapshot at end of quarter
3,000		Selection	1,000
2,500		Qualification	900
3,000		Needs Assessment	750
2,000		Letter of Understanding	740
1,000		Presentation Demo	720
550		Solution Proposal & Technical Check	550
1,000		Production Demo	500
700		Quotation Submission	250
700		Negotiation	170
		Closing	

"Well, Barry, you don't expect me to acknowledge this on the spot. My official party line is that I am running this organization efficiently and professionally." As a matter of fact, I don't see anything special with the numbers. They're just numbers. As expected, the potential is usually greater than the actual exploitation of it. And, of course, the deeper I go in the funnel the lower the numbers drop, but that's expected. I don't see anything, so I am kind of playing dumb here. But, hey, since I decided to give this process a chance, I might as well listen. Luckily, Barry ignores my poor sense of humor. He continues with confidence:

"As you read in the books that I gave you, TOC gives five steps for continuous improvement:

1. *Identify the constraint.*

2. *Exploit the constraint.*

3. *Subordinate all other processes to the constraint.*

4. *Elevate the constraint.*

5. *Start all over again from step one.*"

"So?"

"In many cases, people jump to step four: elevate the limitations created by the existence of the constraint, the organization's bottleneck. But this is often a wrong start, and usually a costly one too. It's usually done by a significant addition of resources. If someone is to do that at your sales organization, it might not turn out to be so easy. If Step Seven is indeed a constraint, adding capacity there isn't a piece of cake. I would guess that your equipment in those demo centers is very expensive. I would also guess that increasing the capital budget for more equipment in the demo centers, in the middle of the year, is out of the question."

"No need for guesses here, Barry. You are absolutely right. I think you know Eliza by now, too."

"Yes, I do. She is one of the top negotiators at this company. In fact, she negotiated my consulting fees. I agree with you, there's no chance for an increase in any budget in the middle of a year. Anyway, let's come back to our case and let's focus on steps two and three above – this may be the best thing to do. There is no time to lose. Step two says: Exploit your constrained resource. In other words, maximize the usage of your bottleneck resource. In your case, you need to find ways to increase the number of demos given per day: expand working hours; add more shifts; find a replacement during lunch time; move some technically capable sales guys from sales to demo; move some customer-support guys with good presentation skills to demo; take your best administrator to manage the scheduling of the demos; see if research and development or engineering can help you with challenging cases. Multiply your demo capacity from two per day to four per day within the next couple of weeks. Focus on that – no excuses!"

"And then?"

"Then go to step three. Subordination to the dictates of the constraints is the most difficult one, and usually the most counterintuitive. It's difficult because unlike the constraint, which is limited to single function or location, subordination must encompass the entire organization. To see how counterintuitive it is, listen to this: do not add more prospects in the funnel unless you have completed more demos. The ratio is to be determined later. In short, don't go through steps one or two, don't make any more selections or qualifications of prospects, unless the production demos are done." Well, counterintuitive it surely is. It also goes against common sense.

"Barry, you must be kidding me. I am pushing my guys to do more cold calls, to dig very deep in the market, not to leave any stone unturned. And I beat them hard when the competition sells without any real competition from us. And what are you saying? 'Don't push in the market anymore.'"

"Roger, let me be blunt. It is pointless to add more prospects to the funnel while you know you'll lose them later on because you can't make a quality demo on time. You are simply wasting your selling resources on steps one to six, while step seven kills them anyhow. If you keep adding prospects into the process you lose visibility of truly important prospects - those that have passed through the bottleneck. You lose focus on the critical steps eight to ten. You should add more prospects into the cycle only at the rate of your bottleneck. Focus on steps eight to ten to close as many prospects as possible post the production demo step."

"And then?"

"Then, and only then, elevate the constraint. Increase your demonstration capacity significantly. When this is done, look for the new constraint. This may be the coverage again, or this may be the market itself which can't take more products because of market saturation, or because your products were made obsolete by some new technology."

"I see. Barry, I am afraid we need to close this session. I guess I have some challenges ahead of me. Let's meet again in two weeks."

"No problem, I'll set it up with Amy."

*   *   *

This is all very nice and simple. The only thing that I didn't mention is that the person in charge of all demo operations is no one else but the VP of Marketing. I held that position not too long ago but now it's Pierce's job. I'm trying to think about how I'm going to explain all of this to Pierce; I know he won't make my life easy. I decide not to lose any time; I go straight to Pierce's office. I hope he'll remember how supportive I was in the Lilly's launch.

"Hi, Pierce. Do you have a few minutes for me?"

"Sure, come in. Am I not supposed to support the new VP of Sales? By the way, just from talking to my ex-guys in the field, it doesn't seem like the situation is improving." Am I sensing some gloating? Well, maybe Pierce is not being very helpful, but he is right. Unfortunately, the situation has further deteriorated since I took over. Without losing any more time, I brief Pierce about the discussion I had with Barry. Fifteen minutes later, I am still talking.

"So, the production demo step is the bottleneck of our sales cycles. I need to exploit that bottleneck better. In other words, we need to find a way to do twice as many production demos with the same amount of resources."

"Roger, you're talking and talking and to be honest, I am not sure if I can believe my own ears. Sales is an art, not a production system. Salesmanship is something you either have, or you'd better turn to another profession. What made me successful over the years is the ability to convince customers to put their signature on a purchase order. For that, I needed an intimate knowledge of their needs and also of their personalities. That art is much closer to psychology than to manufacturing. I am sorry to say this, but you're heading the wrong way."

What I feared the most is happening. I need to turn the situation around; otherwise, this will lead nowhere. My intuition tells me that I have reached a critical milestone.

"Listen, Pierce. There is no contradiction. Producing a magazine page, a printed circuit board, a software module or a car is an art too. It all requires creativity and deep knowledge of certain processes. At the same time, you can relate to it in operational terms. Success comes from mastering both the art and the operational side of this or that business. We need to focus. I believe that our ability to convince customers to buy is an asset we have, or, if you will, an art we master. Right now, the focus is on expanding the global capacity of our sales force to generate more orders, or to close more deals. One can't take care of both angles simultaneously. Now, I want to focus on capacity expansion. This is my choice and I need your help. You manage the bottleneck resource and I will not be able to expand our selling capacity without taking care of what I currently believe is the bottleneck. I am asking for your help, and I need it urgently."

"Roger, if all you need is for me to double the capacity of the demo centers around the country, I'll take care of it. My worry is that this won't be the thing that will save us."

"Pierce, once we solve that one, there will be more constraints that we'll need to take care of. Thanks for your support, but I need more; I need someone to tell me on a weekly basis how many good demos have been made. By that I mean, how many demos were successful enough so that the sales cycle for that specific prospect moves to the next step. This is how I plan to regulate the entry of more qualified prospects in to the funnel with a certain ratio that I still need to determine."

"Roger, I am completely losing you here." It's not cynicism I hear; it's a genuine surprise in his voice. "What do you mean by "regulate". Do you say you want to limit the number of cold calls, or any other lead-generation activities such as shows, open houses and mailers? Are you mad, my friend?"

"No, Pierce, I'm not, but you've got it right – there is absolutely no point in having more leads, when the progress of sales cycles is inhibited by production demos. This simply creates huge work-in-progress that does not turn into closed orders, which is what we need the most now."

"God bless you, Roger. Do whatever you want. And yes, we'll be giving you a weekly report of the amount of successful demos."

"Thanks, Pierce, I appreciate your cooperation."

*   *   *

Here we are three weeks later. I must say that Pierce, although still not convinced, has done a great job. He did it all: increased the hours of operation, brought some older equipment back to operation, brought some equipment from the training rooms to the demo centers and added some personnel from customer support and marketing, I gave him a few people from pre-sales. There is now a national demo coordinator who is able to provide me with the statistics.

I have gathered all four of my Regional Sales Managers in North America. Their District Sales Managers are here with them. All the twelve Sales Managers, whom Pierce used to call his twelve apostles, are in the room. After some small talk, I start.

"Guys, allow me to make the following drawing on the board. You all know it by heart."

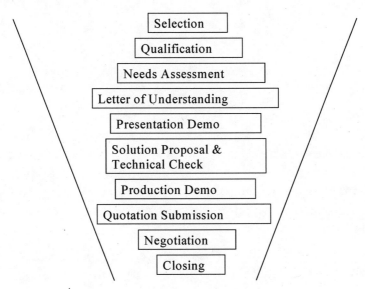

I continue:

"We currently generate orders of around one hundred and twenty million dollars per quarter in North America alone. Our average order is seven hundred thousand dollars. In other words, we generate around one hundred and seventy orders every quarter. Our seventy sales people and twenty reps perform this work. The question is: what is stopping us from doing more. Much more. Chris did some analysis at my request. Look at the numbers."

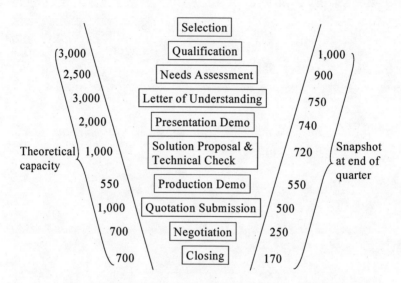

"What do we see here? First of all, looking at the snapshot at the end of last quarter, we can see that while we had one hundred and seventy closed orders, we had a total of more than five thousand prospects in all the other steps together." When I see their surprise, I explain:

"From the numbers we can see that we had 1,000 prospects at the *Qualification* stage, while 900 prospects were in the midst of *Needs Assessment*. Similarly, for 750 prospects a *Letter of Understanding* was in the make. If you add up all the prospects in the various sales stages, you will notice that while we had one hundred and seventy closed orders, we had 5,410 prospects in all the other steps. This is impressive. But what does it show? It shows that the chances of a flat next quarter are very high. We should not expect the average order size to increase. What else does it show?" They don't answer. The numbers must overwhelm them.

Then one of them starts:

"It also shows that more than half of the prospects are immediately lost in the first two or three steps. That makes sense, as certainly some of them aren't really interested in our products. The problem is, that we are losing too many of them in the later steps, after we have already invested of lot of effort in them." This is Eric, our Northwest Regional Sales Manager. He is absolutely right.

Then somebody else stands up:

"I am looking more at the capacity table, I guess that it relates to the aggregate of what all our sales channels could potentially handle at the same time." This is John, our Central Region Sales Manager, and our man in Chicago. I respond:

"You are right. We took many assumptions here, but I think that this is a good ballpark figure."

"Well," John continues, "if this is the case, I have two immediate conclusions. Firstly, we're really wasting time in some of the first steps because even if we are capable of bringing more prospects to the production demo stage, we will end up losing them anyway because there's simply not enough capacity.

"Secondly, we need to make sure that we can make more production demos, otherwise, we can forget about closing more orders." It is so nice to have others see for themselves what you wanted to explain to them in the first place. How come I didn't see this as quickly as they have? And I'm their boss.

"Bingo." I'm trying not to sound too excited. "What you just mentioned is the exact definition of a bottleneck in production terms; or a constraint in more generalized ones. And I have some news for you! With the help of Pierce, your ex-boss, our production demo capacity stands now at about one thousand demos per quarter. That's almost twice as many as we had in the past. This is what we call a much better exploitation of the bottleneck." From then on, I go into a lengthy explanation about why the input to the process needs to be linked to the pace of the bottleneck. They are as astonished as Pierce and I were in the beginning, but at the end they get it. I conclude: "To summarize, you will be asked to link your activities related to *Qualification* and *Needs Assessment* to the actual performance of the *Production Demos*. Any ideas on how to do that?"

"In my case, it shouldn't be too difficult." I'm glad that the District Managers are starting to talk too. Jeff is our presence in the Washington/Oregon area. "My guys and I review our activity on a daily basis. When we see that we don't have enough qualified leads, we push the front-end of the process. Towards the end of the quarter, we definitely push the back-end of the process. Now, we will simply do that based on the amount of production demos. We all know that this is not an exact science, but I think that we can handle this quite well." They all agree. The meeting seems to proceed easily, exceeding all my expectations.

"I have a question" Julie is the Southwest District Manager, covering Texas and Arizona.

"Go ahead, Julie."

"If now we are able to do thousand demos per quarter, it seems that the *Production Demo* is no longer a bottleneck as you call it." Julie is sharp as a razor. I am sure she'll come up with a good question. I hope that I'll find the answer. "If I look at your drawing on the board, the next item that can stop us from achieving our goals is *Solution Proposal* and *Technical Check*. This is mostly done by or with the help of sales support. You see, if we'll be able to run one thousand production demos, this should come after at least thirteen hundred or so solution proposals. Now, according to you, the theoretical capacity is one thousand solution proposals. If we're already here, let's kill that bird, too."

"Julie, the question is excellent. However, we are not there yet. Investing efforts in that step is like investing efforts in a non-bottleneck – it does not generate better end results, i.e. more orders. You see, there are no two bottlenecks in the same production line, there is only one. We need to solve one at the time, and then look at the new interdependencies that are created. We will definitely look at *Solution Proposal* and *Technical Check* again in our next quarterly meeting. Now is simply not the time."

We conclude the meeting by spending several more hours on some business situations. We try to forecast how the quarter will end. I wonder whether the new capacity of the demo centers will have an effect this quarter.

*   *   *

On the way back home, I stop by the coffee bar at the Barnes & Noble just in front of the Burlington Mall. With my Grande Cappuccino in hand, I am better off for the trip home. When I finally arrive home, I realize that Joanna and Lizzie are still out. This is a good opportunity to find out what Jennifer is up to. I find her in her room with Karen, her best friend.

"Hi, Jennifer. Hello Karen. What's up?"

"Dad, you are exactly the person we need!" This is an unusual statement, unless she needs an urgent lift to one of her friends' houses.

"No, Dad, this is not about driving me to Katie's." She's obviously reading my mind. "We have a marketing assignment and luckily, you're an expert."

"Okay, this could be interesting, what's the assignment about?"

"Well, this is an assignment we got from a friend of our teacher. This friend teaches marketing at Boston College. I am doing this with Karen. We kind of volunteered and we are counting on you to help us."

"Nice. So what's the problem then?"

"I have everything mixed up: awareness creation, lead generation, incitement of interest. Dad, please clear it all up for us."

"Wow, I feel like I'm going back twenty years. But basically, this is all very simple. You have two types of products that people buy: spontaneous and rational products. Let's start from the rational products, i.e. products that responsible people buy after some rational decision-making processes. When they need something, they first try to hear about a certain brand, which makes such products. Then they show some interests in that brand, and then they learn about a certain product from that brand. If there is interest to buy it, they become a "lead," or a "good prospect" for the supplier of that brand. The marketing function is responsible to bring as many relevant people or companies to the stage of becoming a lead or a 'hot' prospect. The marketing function is also responsible to identify where the problem is: Awareness? Interest? Knowledge? Once they know, they are able to focus their marketing campaign accordingly."

"Give me an example."

"Mercedes has a great brand awareness. Everybody easily recognizes it. However, most people don't show an interest in Mercedes cars because they believe that those cars are too expensive for them. This is why the Mercedes marketing campaigns emphasize the price of their lower-class models."

"And another one."

"When Whirlpool was established, nobody had ever heard about that name. There was zero awareness. They created a very aggressive campaign just to make people aware of that brand name. They did not provide any information or knowledge, they did not emphasize or generate interest for any specific appliance. At the time, they did a very good job. Now, everybody knows Whirlpool. There is no longer an awareness problem."

"So what about spontaneous products?"

"In spontaneous products, there is no logical order. You see new toothpaste with a nice packaging. First you'll buy it, and then maybe you'll recognize the brand name. After you use it, you may show interest in what is special about this brand. For those types of products, mostly low-cost consumer goods, there is no specific order in the buying process; it is more compli-cated than that. There are many psychological elements in-volved."

Now, when all this stuff, long forgotten, starts to come back to me, I can really go on and on. But it seems that the girls had enough:

"Dad, you really helped us. We can start to summarize it now. We have lots to talk about."

I love my daughter. She is always so serious. I have big hopes for her.

*　　*　　*

Chapter 3
Cost or Throughput?

May 16, Year 2

I am six months on the job now, and Ray, our Chairman, has asked me to meet with him in his office. When Ray founded the company he was more of a technology visionary than a businessman. He knew, many years before it really happened, that the imaging processes would ultimately change to digital, and that the old analog processes would disappear. Like many people of his kind, who were forward thinking and who made zillions of dollars following their intuition, Ray has become quite arrogant, and sometimes he's not very nice to people around him. Although he doesn't have a formal role in the day-to-day running of the company, he still keeps an office here. He comes to work quite frequently, usually to see Gary, and hardly ever bothers to acknowledge the people he sees in the hallway. Ray is definitely not a people-oriented person, to say the least. And to make things worse, he saves me the walk to his office and simply walks into mine: "Hi, Roger, so how are we doing?" Well, this is a loaded question, no doubt. I know he talks to Gary almost daily; he's aware of everything that goes on at Carmen Graphic Solutions. And he certainly knows what's happening to our stock.

"Hi, Ray. As you know, we are now in the middle of Q2. Q1 was our first quarter of growth since the beginning of last year. This was a modest growth, but it is still growth. As Gary may have told you, I have taken a slightly different approach to the selling process. From the District Sales Management level and below, it remains traditional selling: steps-of-sales; relationship management; negotiations; decision-making units; product argumentation and solutions proposal. At my level down to the Regional Sales Managers level it is all that plus a more operational look at sales. By having an operational view on sales, we could start to apply TOC methodologies. So, once we accomplished that, we quickly expanded our selling capacity with virtually the same resources. It helped us in knowing where to invest our attention and our efforts. I must say that Barry Kahn, our 'famous' consultant, should be given a lot of credit for that new approach. The bottom line result is that we are now gaining back market share and our sales are increasing."

"Yes, I heard about the whole process. I am satisfied with the Q1 results, but I hope you understand that this is not enough. I am afraid that you will rest on your laurels. I am sure Gary told you – we are not out of danger yet. We must achieve more and faster. Tell me what you plan on doing next."

I am not really prepared for this. After we announced the Q1 results, I was really happy. Now, I feel exactly like I felt when I was appointed to the VP Sales position. Gosh, I hope he won't notice I'm starting to sweat. "Ray, I am not resting for a second. Not at all. I think that we as a company have a serious problem with deliveries. We have a management meeting this afternoon. Solving that may be our next improvement. This has become my problem, as it hurts my selling ability directly. I plan on raising the issue with John, our VP of Operations, today."

"That's fine. But if that's all you plan to do in order to improve our sales you are still not giving me the confidence of fast-enough improvements. Frankly, I am more concerned now than I was before. I realize that there are always problems with Operations, but that isn't much of a marketing plan. It's just a quick fix of a minor problem, not a solution to our crisis. Roger, to say the truth, I was not in favor of Gary's decision to put you on the job but I let him do it anyway. He is the CEO, after all. As it stands now, I am afraid, he may have made a fatal mistake. A mistake we can't afford now."

This is what I call encouragement. I'm making incredible improvements in a desperate situation, and I am still a fatal mistake. "Ray, I will make no false promises. The decision to keep me on the job is your call, not mine. As long as I am here, I am committed to use all my energy, experience and any other skill to succeed. That's what I can do."

"It's not enough, I want results and fast. This year, we need to be over eight hundred million dollars. The Q1 run rate does not warrant that."

"I hear you loud and clear." There is no point in continuing this discussion. The guy simply does not believe in me, and I don't like him. Truly mutual feelings. I am happy when he leaves my office.

*   *   *

The management meeting is beginning. It isn't easy to be calm after the meeting with Ray, but I don't really have a choice; I have to deal with the problem of our lousy deliveries. So I start: "Gary and John, the deliveries are killing us. We improved our selling ability so much. We are really hurting our competition now. Our market share gained three full percentage points in less than three months. However, now every order is becoming a nightmare. We simply do not meet our delivery times. Our sales guys are dealing more with post-sale or damage-control activities than with pre-sales or business-generation activities. Something must be done. And we'd better do it fast." John is genuinely surprised. He responds:

"I have all the data in front of me. I can assure you, we committed to delivery times of one month and we meet that com-

- 38 -

mitment. I am really proud of my guys. They do an outstanding job." I feel I'm about to burst:

"John, you must be kidding me. Either that or your guys are kidding you. One month my ass. Sixty days at best. I don't know where you're getting your data." Gary quickly jumps in:

"Guys, guys, let's calm down. Let's use some of the methods we have learned. John, let's go through the process slowly. I am sure we have a process here – a sequence of mutually dependent steps that lead from order-taking to delivery. What are those steps?"

"You're right, Gary. Let's calm down. Roger and I have cooperated very nicely in the past. We can do this again. Right, Roger?" What can I say?

"Yes, John, sure. Sorry if I overreacted." I don't know what this job has done to me. Ever since I took Pierce's job, I tend to overreact much like he always did. Am I becoming like him? I hate the mere thought of it.

"Okay, here are the main steps:

1. ***Order received by Order Administration***: Three basic checks: (a) configuration check; (b) deal gross margin; (c) customer financial status.

2. ***Approval cycle***.

3. ***Back to Order Administration*** for equipment allocation from either inventory or production plan.

4. ***Approved order received by Production***: product integration and customization per customer order; testing and packing.

5. ***Order received by Traffic***. Traffic ensures order is properly shipped to destination.

6. ***Order sent back to Order Administration***. Order administration updates installed base database and submits installation call for customer services. That last steps triggers the

installation process that is yet another process that leads to completion of installation (COI). COI triggers the warranty and cash collection processes."

"Thanks, John. Do you have an estimate of how long each of the above six steps takes."

"Very rough. Let's see. Step One takes one day at most. Step Two takes three days if everything goes okay, but may take much longer if, for example, the gross margin does not meet company guidelines. Step Three is one day at most. Step Four is three days if equipment comes from stock, or up to ten days if equipment comes from production plans. Step Five is two days max. Transportation varies but it is three days max. You see, if everything goes right, the whole process is maximum twenty days. We committed to thirty days. Of course, as I said, if Sales sell for low margins, or if they sell to customers who have a low credit rating, the approval cycle may take longer."

It's now becoming clear to me what happens; so clear. How come I didn't see this earlier? It seems that I'm not the only one to see the problem; slowly, Gary asks: "Guys, it seems that we found the constraint of the entire process here. It's the approval step. Let's see – who is on the approval cycle?"

John seems to be very sure: "The Sales Executive, the District Sales Manager and the Regional Sales Manager are the ones who sign on the order before it even comes to Order Admin. After Order Admin., we have the Product Manager, the Financial Controller; you Roger; the VP of Sales, and Eliza, the VP of Finance. If the Gross Margin is below thirty percent, it even comes to you, Gary."

"And what happens when those people are not around?"

"Order Admin. is chasing them. The order can sometimes sit on somebody's desk for a whole week. Or longer!"

"And what would happen without the approval cycle?"

"My initial answer would be that we would sell to customers with low credit rating, or we might have configurations that don't work, or we might sell at a loss. I say that this is my initial answer, but at the same time, in my last three years on the job, I have never actually seen an order that was cancelled! It almost becomes a psychological matter: it may be that because sales people know that orders with a low gross margin go straight to the CEO, we have fewer of those. I don't really know why it is so. I am not so sure. The approval process was established long before I joined CGS."

"I see," says Gary. "Let's adjourn this session. If you guys don't mind, I'll present our findings here to Barry. We'll see what he has to say."

"No problem, Gary," says John quietly.

"Gary and John, thanks for taking the time. Let's try to reach a conclusion as soon as possible. My people extinguish fires due to late deliveries instead of selling. I can't afford that." I am happy to emphasize again how urgent the need is for improvement.

*   *   *

Eliza and I decide to go out for lunch today. It's not very often that I go to a restaurant for lunch, but when the VP of Finance invites you, you had better accept. Especially when she wants to discuss our sales recognition policies.

As we enter a nice little Italian restaurant in Bedford, I am surprised to see Ray and Pierce having lunch together at another table. It seems like they are having a heated discussion. I wonder what those guys are talking about. I know that Ray and Pierce go a long way back together. When Ray was CEO, Pierce was the best Regional Sales Manager he had. I am sure if the business hadn't deteriorated last year, Pierce would have been next in line to inherit the CEO position. Ever since Gary appointed me to the VP Sales position, they seem to both be waiting for my failure.

Unfortunately, or fortunately, I don't know how to think anymore, I am doing quite well. The company is really doing better every quarter. Pierce had been managing Sales by being the best sales person in the team and even more – the best closer. I am not focusing on that at all. Luckily, the Regional Sales Managers are good at that – they don't really need me at all. From my position, I have been able to orchestrate everything around throughput management and bring in more orders more efficiently. Exploit and elevate constraints. This may seem boring and less creative, but surprisingly, it surely works. And it works damned well.

Is Pierce panicking? What about Ray? The share is back above $25 and he is a major shareholder! I approach them and shake Ray's hand. They both seem a bit embarrassed to see me. They ask Eliza and me to join them, but we find a lame reason to be excused. We leave them there and find a table on the other side of the restaurant.

Eliza and I discuss the issues around revenue recognition policies. It's Eliza, not me, who determines the extent of our sales, after all, and Eliza is very conservative. Every quarter, she – as CFO – increases the provisions for bad debt. In simple terms, this means that not all the sales our people make are recognized as such. This, in turn, means that I need to bring even more orders than the target just to compensate for all those endless, and I must admit, frustrating, provisions. Eliza explains her point of view. She is at least very consistent. She sees her task as protecting me, as well as all members of management. She protects us from potential revenue cancellations caused by some customers failing to pay for what they bought from CGS. She talks about risk management and about company integrity. She mentions Enron and Worldcom. She explains how the SEC reacts today to any suspicion of improper accounting. This is all well and good. I guess that this is part of the checks and balances in a company. It's just that now that I am in charge of Sales, every dollar that comes in is a fight, and every dollar that is then taken away leaves a sour taste in my mouth. I am sure she knows that, but we all have our jobs to do. Surely she does hers very well. I finish my conversation quite frustrated; she isn't going to budge even one inch on her policies. We simply have to bring in even more sales.

*   *   *

As Gary promised, we are gathered again in the management conference room to discuss the late deliveries. Gary briefed Barry before the meeting. It seems that Barry may have an answer to that too. After a short introduction by Gary, the podium is handed over to Barry.

"We have a very common dilemma. It's what I call the war of *in-process* cost control vs. *out-of process* cost prevention. This is not simple to solve and the debate will probably go on forever. In simple words: *in-process* cost control consists typically of measures taken to control, or decrease, the costs of a business cycle. Those measures are mandatory steps in the business cycle and cannot be avoided. The most typical example is the signature or approval of the CFO prior to a purchase, as an integral part of the purchasing cycle. Of course, each such step may add to the duration of the process, sometimes considerably. But it definitely contributes to savings, by preventing unnecessary expenses. There are many more examples of it.

"On the other hand there is another approach, *out-of-process* cost prevention consists of measures taken outside of the business cycle. They are not mandatory steps within the cycle and they cannot stop the process. As such, they don't prolong it, but because they aren't part of the mandatory process they may come too late, after the unnecessary expense was incurred.

Those measures are also taken to reduce costs or to prevent unnecessary expenses, but because they aren't part of the mandatory process, as I've said, they don't prolong its duration. A typical example is the creation of a black list of customers. Sales is not allowed to take orders from customers on the black list because they are, for example, defaulting on payments. How did we find out they were a bad risk? After they didn't pay us in the past! We've paid a significant price to discover that. Now it's after the fact, but at least we want to prevent that from happening again. Is our dilemma clear?"

"Absolutely!" John is the first to react.

"Yep," reacts Gary, as usual.

"In TOC, we often talk about the 'throughput' world vs. the 'cost' world. Cost-oriented people will advocate the *in-process* control method. Throughput-oriented managers will most often opt for *out-of-process* cost prevention. Before I make any recommendation, I need to draw the conflict below on the board."

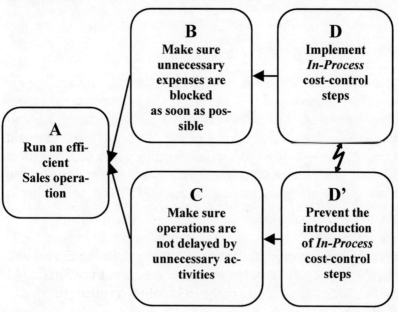

And Barry continues:

"The way you have to read is: in order to **A**…. you have to **B**…. For example: in order to 'Run an efficient sales operation' you have to 'Make sure unnecessary expenses are blocked as soon as possible,' and to do that, you need to implement 'In-process cost control steps.'"

"Well," Gary is first to react, "what you have done so far is to merely verbalize what you said before, but now it's presented more concisely, correct?"

"Exactly," Barry is quick to respond, "but please be patient. Now, let's use the word 'really' and see if our underlying assumptions are correct. Often things exist because of inertia, and not because of good reasons. So let's try. When talking about the approval cycle for new orders, in order to 'make sure unnecessary expenses are blocked as soon as possible,' you REALLY need to introduce 'In-process cost control.'"

"No!" I am first to jump in here. "We all heard it from John himself. Didn't he say that in his last three years on the job, he had never seen an order cancelled? The in-process control like you call it does not REALLY ensure that unnecessary expenses are blocked. It has become part of our inertia."

"Right!" interjects Barry. "May I suggest that you move immediately to out-of-process prevention? Make sure Order Administration has a list of customers that are not credit worthy; that it provides timely feedback to management on low margin orders so that they make sure by managerial means that such orders do not happen again; that we provide adequate configuration tools as close as possible to the field so that your guys sell solutions that work."

"Barry, I have a question." John is now back in the discussion. "Should we now move to out-of-process intervention in all cases? What you're saying makes a lot of sense after all."

"No, John. Sometimes, 'Really' is really real! For example: When talking about the approval cycle for new capital purchases above this or that amount, in order to 'make sure unnecessary expenses are blocked as soon as possible,' you REALLY need to implement 'in-process cost control.' Here, the answer is positive. Sometimes management or finance really causes you to avoid bad purchases. Here, in-process cost control is valid and required."

"I see." John starts to lighten up. "If we do that, we now have a potential saving of two to twenty, or even sometimes thirty days. That's what I call a good and productive meeting. What's next?"

Gary is first to respond, "You all know the answers. We elevated the current constraint, and now we need to simply identify the next one. If we push it, we could probably go under ten days from order to delivery."

Barry tries to cool things down: "Let's do things one at the time. Are you all going to watch the game tonight?"

Without too much hope, I answer him: "Sure, I'm hoping that the Red Socks will win their first game this season. I am counting on that."

"Okay, guys. Back to work."

*   *   *

As I get home, Joanna tells me to urgently call my Dad. She says he was pretty upset when he called.

"Hi, Dad, this is Roger. Joanna said you called earlier. So here I am."

"Hi, son, thanks for calling back. Listen, your Mom and I are really worried about your sister. You know she has this boyfriend we really don't like. He definitely isn't Mr. Right. At least not for her. It seems now that she's falling in love with the guy. We love Michelle so much. I am afraid she is going to get hurt."

"Dad, you don't want me to interfere, do you?" Michelle is the youngest in our family. But she is twenty-five now. She's supposed to make decisions on her own, isn't she?

"Yes, but Roger, I am asking this as a personal favor. You know, I've never really asked anything like this from you before, but now I want you to do something about this. I want you to talk to her. She won't listen to her parents anymore. I am asking for your help. You must help your sister."

"Dad, you know I would do anything for you, but before I talk to her, let me think about it, and let's talk about it again during the weekend."

"Okay, but don't forget. By the time you talk to her, it might already be too late."

"Dad, I promise."

*　　　*　　　*

Eliza steps into my office. Without as much as a word of small talk, she goes straight to business: "Hi Roger. Do you want to know how Bob, my Controller, reacted when I told him that he was a bottleneck in the delivery cycle and therefore he would no longer need to approve all orders?"

That's the last thing I need now; another disheartened person in the sales loop. Well, after Gary's decision, not so much in the loop. "My God, Eliza, I hope you didn't present it to him that way."

"Well, you know, I am the direct type. The approval cycle is a manifest constraint in our process. We need to elevate it. Period. Bob was in the way. Bob is no longer in the way. End of story." Indeed, she is a direct person. Too direct one may say.

"Eliza, Eliza, this is counterproductive. We all need Bob to continue protecting the business as he has always done. The only thing is that we need him to focus on the 'post-mortem' control steps, rather than being part of the process. In doing that he is still able to prevent future damage from materializing. Also, we must be very sensitive – being part of the approval cycle is a source of power, after all. Eliza, do you mind if we ask Bob to join us. I'd like to explain this to him myself, while you're here. Okay?"

"Sure, let me bring some coffee, too. Do you want some?"

"Columbian Supremo, a little milk, no sugar. Thanks!"

Eliza comes in with Bob and coffee for all of us. Bob looks like a beaten animal. After all these years, the poor guy has not gotten used to Eliza's harsh style.

"Bob, let me ask you a few questions, okay?"

"Go ahead Roger, I am all yours." Uhh, I hate that kind of statement. What does it mean 'I'm all yours'? It seems that the guy is not only beaten but has also surrendered.

"In all the years you've been approving incoming orders, how many of them have you stopped?"

"Roger, I know where you're coming from. You are right; very few. But I have called Sales Managers or Sales Executives, or even Gary, you or Pierce regarding unacceptable commitments made by Sales in certain orders very often. I feel like I am the company's gatekeeper. People know that I will be calling them and asking tough questions. They know that I will not hesitate to 'report them' to management. It is the built-in fear factor that I'm establishing that's protecting our business. It will disappear if this process is eliminated. Believe me, I know what I'm talking about."

"Bob, let's take it step by step. I fully understand what you're saying. How long do you hold the orders on average?"

"When I'm in the office, it's a twenty-four-hour turnaround time. Sometimes I need to go to the bank or to one of our branches to close a leasing deal. It can then wait a few days. I would still say not more than three days, with an average close to thirty-six hours."

I continue: "When you encounter a problematic order, either low margin or a customer with a problematic credit rating or bad paying habits, what do you do then?"

"I call the Regional Sales Manager. As I said before, I kind of establish a fear factor so that such bad business does not happen again. I often inform you or Gary, too. Eliza is always in the loop."

"How long do you hold onto the order then?"

"For those ugly orders it can take up to a week. In rare cases, even longer."

"How many orders do you have lying on your desk now?"

"I've got a big pile of them today. Probably between thirty and fifty."

"What do you do at quarter end?"

"At quarter end we are under huge pressure to deliver and I don't want to delay the process. I know what end-of-the-quarter sales figures mean for the company. So I sign the orders automatically and I make copies of the problematic ones. I deal with those after quarter end."

I see that he is quite a smart guy. "Bob, this is it. That's the solution! You see, once we have established that the approval cycle is the bottleneck, this means that the delivery process is stuck if the bottleneck capacity is not fully exploited or elevated. This means that the bottleneck resource is always under pressure. I want to emphasize the word 'always'; in other words, not just at quarter end. When an operation is not run, or timed, by a bottleneck, the bottleneck is often not visible. There are many open orders in the system; there are stocks of work-in-process everywhere. What I am asking you to do is exactly what you've always done: be the company's gatekeeper; protect the business; create the fear-factor for bad business. I still want you to get copies of all orders, but deal with them all after the fact, like you do now with end-of-quarter orders. By all means, I repeat, do it!"

"And what about the orders that I used to stop, the ones that we knew customers would not be capable of paying?"

"Bob, take preventive measures. Establish the black list – a list of customers that we should not accept orders from without your prior approval and that of Eliza. Set the process; I will support it. Hand the list over to the Order Administrators. What percentage of customers are we talking about?"

"I would say less than one percent."

"Bob, isn't it a no-brainer?"

"You may be right. Let's give it a try. We'll see how it goes."

"Thanks, Bob, thanks, Eliza. Thanks for the coffee."

*　　　*　　　*

Eric, our Northwest Regional Sales Manager, is on the line. He calls from San Jose, California. "Roger, I don't how to say this. We've been working together for several months now. I think we get along quite well. But now I have a problem. It's rather delicate."

"Go on," I tell Eric, "You know that I like direct communication. This is what you get from me, and this is what I deserve from you."

"Well, Roger, this is about Pierce. I think that he is talking to some of my bigger customers."

"So? I don't see any problem with that. He is our VP of Marketing. Those customers are an important source of input. I used to talk to customers too when I was in that position." I try to sound as impartial as possible. The UN secretary general doesn't sound more impartial. What the hell is Pierce up to now?

"The problem is not that he is talking, the problem is the nature of those conversations."

"What do you mean, Eric?"

"I mean that he's acting like the VP of Sales, instead of the VP of Marketing. He tries to close deals. He sets terms of payments like price, or warranty period – everything. Whenever I am back with that account, I am facing facts that I can do nothing to change or improve. I'm facing a done deal."

"You mean that he did not even coordinate that with you?"

"No. He used to do this before, but he was the boss then. I thought that with you, this would no longer be the case."

"I see. Thanks, Eric, I appreciate your calling me. I will handle it. And Eric, I would appreciate it if this conversation remains between the two of us. I simply don't want to start a public pissing contest here."

"You have nothing to worry about, Roger. This discussion never happened."

I make a few more phone calls. Then I talk to all my guys. It doesn't take long before I realize that Pierce is doing things behind my back. That's Pierce. What did I expect from this snake? I need to think about the right way to handle this.

*　　*　　*

The discussion with Barry on the in-process *versus* out-of-process control system gave me an idea for my discussion with my dad over the weekend. That it is a crucial issue for him was very evident when I tried to set a time to meet him. Before I could say a word he told me it was about time for him to see his grandchildren, so he and mom will stay with us the coming weekend.

And here he is. "Dad, it's really great that you and mom came for the whole weekend. I know that you're really eager to talk about Michelle, so let's sit down and have a few words."

"I am with you. Do you have one of those Japanese beers in the fridge?"

"There is plenty of Sapporo's left. Serve yourself and let's sit here together."

"Dad, I've done my homework. I've actually used some of the tools I use in my work to solve the problems." My dad is very proud of me, I know.

"I prepared the following chart. This is a chart that supposedly helps to solve dilemmas. Our current dilemma is whether or not to interfere in Michelle's life. Look at the right-hand side. Is this an accurate description of the dilemma?"

I read the statements very carefully from the chart.

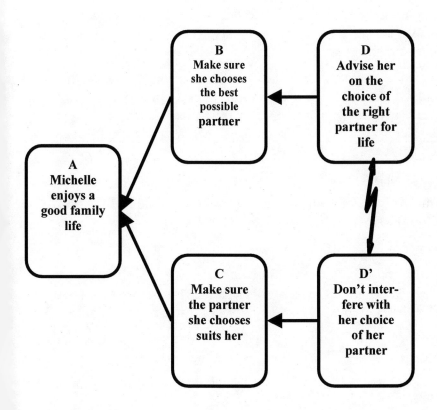

But he doesn't listen at all. "Roger, for me there is no dilemma, I asked you to go and talk to your sister. Why do you make such a big deal out of such a simple request? Can't you simply do what I ask?"

"Dad, please be patient. I am not sure at all what to do. At least, I believe that there is a dilemma. Let's talk about it while you're having your Sapporo. Okay?"

"Okay. Go ahead."

"In the chart that I prepared, you can go from right to left as follows: 'In order for Michelle to have a good family life, she needs to choose the best possible partner.'" When I see he impatiently nods, I continue: "'In order for her to choose the best possible partner, she needs to have your advice on how to choose the right partner for life.'"

"Yes," my dad says, "and that's my advice: let her leave that maggot." I say nothing to make him think I agree; I just move on and say: "So let's continue: 'In order for Michelle to have a good family life, she needs to choose her partner for life based upon her feelings of love.' So far so good?"

"Yes. You can proceed."

"Now, dad, let's be very honest with ourselves and add the simple word REALLY in few places. Okay?"

"Okay."

"So, here we go: 'In order for Michelle to be happily married, she REALLY needs to choose her partner for life based on her real feelings of love'. This sounds okay for me; for you too?"

"She indeed needs to love her partner in order to have a happy marriage and a good life. I concur with that one."

"The next one is: 'In order for Michelle to choose the best possible partner, she REALLY needs your advice on the choice of the right partner for life.' And now, dad, does she REALLY need your advice, guidance and direction in her search for the right partner? Is it always necessary? For everybody? Would it be right for you all the time? What do you think?" He is quiet for a moment. Then he slowly replies:

"Well, to be honest, son, I can't say that I always agree with that one. I myself have been happily married with your mom for nearly forty-five years now and this did not at all depend on some guidance and direction. Nobody gave me that advice, just my heart. And it turned out pretty well. No, this is not necessarily a pre-requisite."

"You are absolutely right, dad. That assumption is wrong, and when you ask me to interfere with Michelle's life, you base this on an underlying assumption that is simply not correct. You see, Michelle is a grown-up and mature woman. If we put too much pressure on her regarding her boyfriend, she'll be blinded by it instead of being positively influenced. And if, in the end, she gets married to that guy anyway, they both will never forget the negative influence. Dad, let it go. Let Michelle run her own life. Don't ask me to interfere." He is silent. He thinks for a minute. Then he hesitantly says:

"You may be right, Roger. Perhaps we should let it go. You are right. Michelle is a smart lady. She'll do what's good for her. At least, let's hope so."

*   *   *

Chapter 4
Critical Implementations

July 31, Year 2

In a few months, this October, I will be running Sales for a full year. It's summer now. The summer in the Boston area this year is sweltering. Last year, we installed central air-conditioning in our home, after what I call 'years of sweating and suffering.' But during the really hot days, it does not suffice, and I close myself off in the bedroom that has an additional wall unit.

Now that I'm beginning to cool off, I start thinking about the wonderful time Jennifer and I had together this past weekend. We went swimming in Walden Pond near Concord. We swam completely around the perimeter of the pond. I don't know how many miles it is around the pond, but I know my legs will be feeling it for quite a long time. It seems that Jennifer is in much better shape than I am.

I love those kind of private activities with my daughters. I have really traveled a lot lately and I feel like I'm losing touch with my own family, which bothers me a lot. When I am away and I call home, I find myself and Jennifer involved in meaningless conversation such as: "How are you doing at school?" "How was your week?" "Did you have a lot of homework?" You can all guess what the answers are: fine, fine and no. This is what I call maintenance talks. What I am looking for while swimming with my daughter is personal talk. I want to know what really goes on in the mind of my own daughter. She has really matured lately; I mean physically. She is already much more of a woman than a teenager. Believe me, this is quite scary for a father.

After some more maintenance talk, I make a first attempt for some more personal talk.

"Jennifer, do some of your close girlfriends already have boyfriends?" I ask. Uhh, this is a loaded question.

"Sure, dad. Karen dates a guy from the twelfth grade. I think that she really is in love with the guy."

"And how do you feel about it? Has it affected your relationships?" She looks at me, surprised:

"Dad, that's the kind of a question mom asks, not you". But then she answers: "In some ways, I guess, it did affect it. We see each other less often now, as she spends a lot of time with Bill. But we do talk over the phone almost daily."

Of course, I have the phone bills to prove it. Two teenagers in the same household is great business for the telephone company.

"Do you envy her? Is there any pressure put on the other girls to find a date too?"

"In a way, there is, but I kind of try not to let it bother me. You know what I mean, don't you? Mom says that when the time is right, it will happen. It's better not to hurry these things."

"You have a wise mom."

"I know, dad. Mom and I get along very well, which is pretty unusual among most of my friends."

"I have seen how you and mom get along, and I must say that this is really a joy for me. What saddens me a little though is that you and Lizzie tend to have quite a lot of bad days."

"I know, dad. But you know how Lizzie is. She is so stubborn. She wants everything to be done her way, and her way only."

"I know, but somehow, I would like the two of you to get along better. After all, you are sisters and you will always be able to count on one another. This means a lot."

"I know, dad. Things are not that bad though. We have good days too."

We continue swimming and talking like that for well over an hour. This is great time, and fun, too. I am so happy, and quite surprised that Jennifer allows that type of personal talk to take place. Not too long ago, she would have stopped me after the first sentence. She is really maturing. That's nice and a bit scary at the same time!

*   *   *

The management team of CGS gathers in the management conference room for its weekly meeting. We are all there. Gary just came back from a tour of our largest customers. He is in the middle of his tour summary, when he points to Tim, our VP of Customer Support.

"We did it all. We increased our bookings, and have elevated bottlenecks in the selling process. We truly shortened the delivery time. We are becoming the clear leader in our market. At the same time, after completing a tour of all our large customers, I'm seeing a problem that I can summarize in a simple sentence. We never – and I mean it – never, ever complete our installation projects on time." A charged silence suddenly fills the room. But Gary sounds very sure of the facts.

He continues: "All these improvements we did are all well and good, but those systematic delays make our customers think twice, even three times, before they consider a repeat purchase.

And sometimes some of them just give up. Now this may sound like a minor issue, but once we have become a market leader and our installed base has grown to the levels we have reached so far, repeat business becomes the main business. Tim, what do you have to say about this? I want clear answers here. Don't BS me."

No need to ever worry about Tim; he's mister nice guy; he'll always find a polite way to respond: "Well, Gary, I see that you have put me on the hot spot here. You are right, though. If I can summarize it in a nutshell, our implementation projects should take four weeks on average, but they usually take longer; we sometimes don't complete an implementation project for two months!"

"Well," I am back in the discussion, "I don't want to push it too far, but allow me to add that the end result is often different from the expectations we set in the selling process. I could say that our solutions, though they work, don't often meet the specs in the contract! And certainly they don't meet our customers' expectations."

"Gary and Roger, I can't honestly dispute the facts." Tim, ever the diplomat. "What I will also tell you is that I believe that most of the core reasons are exogenous to the Customer Support organization. In simple words, there is not a lot we can do. Perhaps we should start selling with three-month implementation projects."

"Tim, forget it," I jump in. "Our competition will kill us. Moreover, our beloved customers will never pay for that. I am sorry to say this, but we absolutely have to – I repeat – have to, find a way to finish on time, in a month or even less."

"Roger, Roger. Theories and dreams are very nice, but we have to deal with reality."

This mister nice guy is really starting to get on my nerves. Trying to sound level-headed, I turn to explain some basic facts to him: "You know, there used to be days when people would say that it would take three months to manufacture a car. This was the unshakable truth of the car-manufacturing world. The last I heard, it was a few days, and I am talking about a single-digit number here."

Gary, always the salesman, tries to pacify us all: "Tim, let's calm down. Take a few days; try to put on the board all the reasons why our projects take so long. I'll have Barry join us. We have already overcome more significant problems; we can win here is as well."

"Makes sense, Gary. Will do!" – Tim flashes his smile. We all agree to meet on Monday morning after the weekend. There isn't much time to waste.

*   *   *

It's Monday already and CGS' management team is meeting for the entire morning to try and solve the installation problems. It's rare that Gary would convene all the managers together when dealing with a problem at a particular function. Usually he sits with the person in charge of such a problem and resolves it in his quiet, balanced way. I wonder what's going on? Maybe Ray is giving him hell, too? Never thought about it. Who knows? Gary is starting the meeting promptly as usual.

"So here we are. The issue at hand is shortening our implementation projects from three months to four weeks, or maybe even less. It's something we must do, if we are to continue to lead the market. Barry, our TOC consultant, will be sitting in with us today as our special guest. Tim, the podium is yours." Tim gives his convincing look:

"Okay guys, most of our implementation projects can be split into six distinct steps:
1. Unpacking

2. Installation of separate stations
3. Networking of all stations
4. Application and workflow set-up
5. Customer training
6. Acceptance test

Usually, steps 1, 2 and 3 are done in parallel, while steps 4, 5 and 6 are usually sequential."

"So far, so good, Tim. Tell us about the problems." Gary likes the meetings to be short and to the point. So Tim continues:

"I can summarize the main causes for delays as follows: 1. There is almost always one station that does not function as it should, or even worse, it simply doesn't work at all; the technical specialist, of that specific station who can bring it up to speed, is often unavailable as per the schedule. He, or she, is unavailable mostly because another project at which he works is being delayed, and we are already in crisis mode. A delay in the completion of step 2 for any single station does not enable the completion of steps 3 and 4, and then of steps 5 and 6. In other words, no customer training and no acceptance test!

2. The customer is not as ready as he should be according to the very clear and very detailed Site Preparation Guide he got from us. Problems go from electricity, through cables for networking, to availability of operators for the training portion of the deal.

3. In Step 6, the Acceptance Test, we sometimes discover that the Application set-up done in Step 4 does not fully meet the customer requirements, and we need to take corrective measures, and that can often take a very long time. As you can see, all these reasons are facts of life that can almost not be avoided."

"I agree that problems are unavoidable, but I will claim here that you can shorten the process by half very quickly!" Barry seems very self-confident.

"Barry, what you're saying sounds ridiculous, and I'm trying to keep my composure here. However, I'll admit that you've had great success with us over the last few years, albeit in an area very far removed from the implementation of projects. So, I'll give you the benefit of the doubt and will let you continue. I am in listening mode, ready to be convinced," says Tim in a very unconvincing tone.

Well, is Mr. Nice Guy losing it? I think to myself. Barry continues:

"Thanks, Tim. You see, any project is a sequence of dependable events. The uncertainty for every event is built-in. So far, you have been the victim of those so-called surprises. The uncertainty should not be ignored. It needs to be managed."

"You have all our attention." Gary leads the discussion now.

"Let me start with a simple question: do you have a project scheduler or a project manager?"

"Of course, every installation is planned well ahead. We use Microsoft Project. We provide the project chart to the customer before starting."

"Good. How much time do you give per step?"

"Well, we give ample time for each step because, as I said, we do not know in advance where the problem will be. You realize that the last thing we want is to be seen by the customer as exceeding the confines of the plan. "

"In other words, you put in a lot of safety; for every single step."

"Well, I'm not sure about a lot, but some safety, yes, sure. By the way, if you ask my people the same question they will deny there is any safety; they will say that the times assigned are the times needed."

"Tim, that's the problem! Experience shows that a step will almost never end ahead of time, before all its safety time is eaten up. The reasons are plenty; some of them are the ones you've pointed out. Others are mostly psychological: there is what we call 'the student syndrome.' As you know, no matter how long before they know about it, most students don't start preparing for exams until the last minute. Then there is the 'software engineer syndrome,' that is; if there's time, there's always a way to make it better; more elegant; more efficient. People feel that if they have more time, they should use it! The safety times added to all of the steps are a mistake."

"But you yourself have admitted that there are often mishaps," Tim remarks. "So what do you recommend in order to deal with these?"

Barry sounds very resolute: "Remove all safety from the distinct steps. Try to put all the safety times as an aggregated buffer at the end of the whole project. You can also put some buffer time in front of processes or steps that use scarce resources, like those very unique specialists that you have just a few of." Seeing the glassy look in Tim's eyes, Barry continues: " Let's see. Tim, give me the typical times that you allocate for all six steps."

"Well," Tim starts. "I would assume the following averages:
1. Unpacking and preparing for installation – 2 days
2. Installation of separate stations – 4 days
3. Networking of all stations – 2 days
4. Application and workflow set-up – 4 days
5. Customer training – 4 days
6. Acceptance test – 4 days.
Total is 20 working days, or 4 weeks."

Barry seems to be very sure of himself: "Tim, this is what you'll do from now on. You'll assign following times:
1. Unpacking – 1 day
2. Installation of separate stations- 2 days
3. Networking of all stations – 1 day
*** Intermediate buffer of 4 days

4. Application and workflow set-up – 2 days
5. Customer training – 2 days
6. Acceptance test – 2 days
*** Project buffer of 6 days.
The total remains 20 days. Just that all steps are now much shorter! There are no buffers set for every single step."

Tim interrupts: "Don't you think we should rather hide the fact that we have buffers somewhere else?"

"Not at all," explains Barry, "first, because people will find it out anyhow, and second, you've said your guys are all professionals and behave professionally. Still, you should tell them that they have two days to install a station, not four, as it used to be. If this causes a problem, you will analyze why, and take the proper corrective actions. Tell them that there is no punishment for being late, as we all know that you left them no safety time at all. Consequently, this is the new goal, and you expect people to meet that goal. You'll see how it works. No more perfectionism as we saw with the software engineer syndrome, and no more delaying starts like in the student syndrome."

"Barry," Gary was again the first to recover, "you promised to shorten the time."

What a guy, I think to myself. Being on time isn't good enough for him; he wants it to be even shorter than that.

It seems that Barry likes that comment less than me: "Gary, before we shorten the times the first goal is to be on time. See what happens here, for example: you have six days to recover from a mistake in the Acceptance Test, regardless of whether you or the customer is faulty. Being on time is a great achievement per se. Once this happens, you can start managing your buffer times and in some cases assign even a shorter time for some steps. Try it. You'll see."

"Tim?"

"Yes, I think I get the idea. Let me bring it up with my people."

"Okay. That was another good meeting. Thanks!"

* * *

Before the meeting ends, I ask Pierce to stay a little longer in the conference room. I have decided to confront him regarding the fact that he operates behind my back on my own turf.

"Pierce, I know that you are closing deals, or at least trying to, without any coordination with me or with the people who report to me now. I want this to stop immediately."

"Roger, Roger. Please calm down a little a bit. Perhaps it's time to face reality here. My dear friend and colleague, the reason I am still here is that people like Ray know the simple truth: it is relationships that build sales, and I own these relationships, so I am in a certain way compensating for what you nearly don't have at all."

"Do you mean that Ray has asked you to interfere in an explicit manner?" I shout back.

"Roger, you are really becoming childish. Do you expect a direct answer from me on that question? Come on. Let's face it. You need me more than I need you. You can hold the title, that's okay. I will bring the business like I have always done. This is my forte."

"Pierce, yes, I do need you – you are right, but not to the extent that you may think. My choice is very simple: I prefer not to have you around at all, rather than have you interfering in an uncoordinated manner. Let me be very blunt: back off of my business. If Ray has something to say, he has my phone number."

"Are you threatening me?"

"Absolutely. I am!"

I stand up and leave the room. There is nothing more to say.

*   *   *

Here I am in the air again, on a flight to Toronto, Canada. In Canada, we work mostly with resellers. I am heading to meet the President of *Imagine*, our Canadian reseller in the Toronto area. The man's name is Chuck Shawn. He's pretty sharp. More than that, he has an excellent relationship with our Toronto customers. My flight is uneventful. There is nothing better one can say about a flight.

I take my rental car and head to the offices of *Imagine*. Toronto is similar to most US cities. The main difference that always strikes me is that the exits off the highways are not numbered sequentially. The exit numbers represent the number of kilometers from a certain starting point. And they use kilometers instead of good, old miles. After a twenty-minute drive, I pull into the visitor's parking spot.

Chuck and I have a nice chat. We go over the numbers as usual. *Imagine* is doing very well. The Toronto market is quite small, but very stable. The business stream from *Imagine* is steady and growing. After a while, I ask, as usual, if there is any way we, CGS, could do something to help *Imagine* generate even more business.

"Well, Roger, I think that the biggest complaint here is that it takes much too long for your sales support staff to review proposals, or to propose technical solutions, such as configurations with multiple stations in an already complex environment."

"What? Can you elaborate, Chuck?"

"You know, I am not involved with all the details. My perception is that we rely heavily on you to help us, especially from the technical, or from the application point of view. So my people send e-mails to you with some type of requests. Unfortunately, they often describe CGS as a black hole. Requests are sent, but nothing comes back unless they call one hundred times or so."

"Well received, Chuck. I'll see what I can do and come back to you. I promise."

We go on and review large prospects for this quarter. Later in the evening, Chuck and I have dinner with an unhappy customer. It's good to have happy customers, but in a way, it is the unhappy ones that drive us to improve. Before going to sleep that night, I call Joanna. Jennifer is still awake and we chat for a while. I then leave a voicemail for our Chuck at CGS. Chuck works for me and he coordinates the work of all sales support functions in Sales. The sales support guys report to their District Sales Manager. Chuck has more of a national coordination role. At the message I brief Chuck about my conversation with the Canadian Chuck. This is another topic I want to solve quickly. No time to lose. Besides, if I don't solve it, Pierce might somehow steer this information to Ray, and then...

*　　　*　　　*

Chapter 5
Healthy Launches

August 15, Year 2

Eliza has gathered us all in the management conference room. This is very rare. Eliza usually prefers to work one on one. Eliza is first to talk. "We have a serious problem. Nine months ago CGS announced its new line of color scanners, the Lilly. With a big splash. You don't want to know how much it cost us. But we received tons of orders, and we've shipped over one hundred Lilly's at this point. But guess what? We are systematically unable to collect cash for those systems. This is becoming an emergency situation."

Eliza is really upset. I can see that on her face. What a disappointment for me. I was so proud of myself and of the team. We really hit the competition with the new Lilly. It is true, though, that I have not seen many repeat sales and customers continuously complain about the product performance.

Tim is next to respond. "That is not a surprise for me. You don't see cash, because we don't get an acceptance from customers. The system simply does not perform as it should." Well, well, well, what we have on table is clearly an attack on Engineering. Let's see what Ron has to say. He is fast to rise in defense:

"The Lilly system works just fine. Unfortunately, I must say that Sales is simply raising expectations too high, and the installation engineers are unable to install and train the customers properly." This is finger-pointing at its best. And they are pointing at Tim and me. I would have hoped that our management team was now immune to that kind of phenomenon. Luckily, Gary is a good leader. I don't have to respond, and he'll be able to sort it out.

"I am sure that Eliza didn't gather us all here to develop a bunch of excuses. We are paid to do good business and to generate cash, not to have fun. Roger, what do you think?"

"I think that the launch of the Lilly was premature. I think that we can't continue to do this, I mean product launches, over and over again the wrong way."

"This deserves a better explanation." Gary will not let it go that easily.

"If I may, I'll use Barry's method to describe conflicts and perhaps I can explain it all better in that way." I take a marker and go to the board. I kind of feel I'm taking over Eliza's meeting but I think it's for a good cause. "We launched the Lilly in the traditional way: we have taken the schedule from Engineering, and – driven by fear of competition – we have announced the product and taken orders as early as we could. Add to that the fact that since our orders for the older generation of scanners declined faster than expected, we at Sales wanted to fill in the gap with the new product as quickly as we possibly could."

"So, what's wrong with that? This is all driven by our efforts to maximize our business potential and fight competition, isn't it?" Pierce is after me, but I have become used to it. After all, the problems lie perhaps with Engineering or Customer Support or even Sales, but he is the one that managed the launch from the marketing point of view, and he is also partly to blame. I choose to ignore him and continue.

"So the sequence is that:

(1) Schedule from Engineering;

(2) Official announcement;

(3) Customer tests or beta sites;

(4) One month after announcement, full customer availability: sell, ship and install as many systems as possible.

The other side of the coin is to refrain from sales until the new product has been proven absolutely reliable. This side of the coin says "delay as much as needed," until you are confident that the product will be accepted, and hence, that cash will be collected. Let me draw the conflict on the board."

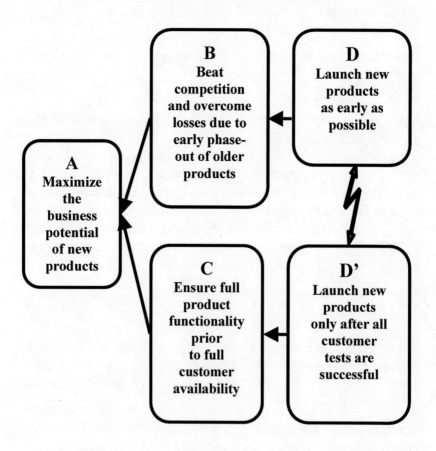

"Now let's see if and where we can add the word REALLY. 'If we want to maximize the business potential, we REALLY need to make sure that we have full product functionality prior to full customer availability.' I think that that statement speaks for itself. No functionality, no acceptance, no cash. With no cash, all efforts made to generate the cash are simply wasted!

"Let's try another one: 'If we want to maximize the business potential, we REALLY need to beat the competition and overcome loss of business due to early phase-out of older generation.' This one is strong too. I see no other way. Let's continue. 'If we want to beat the competition and overcome loss of business due to early phase-out of older generation, we REALLY need to have an early launch.'" I purposely repeat that last one. I hope that somebody will catch it.

"I am not that sure that this is absolutely correct." I am lucky. Eliza is the sharpest one.

"Why?"

"Because if you have an early launch that is premature in terms of product readiness, the competition catches on very quickly and then they can use it against you in the marketplace. Also, if the product does not generate cash, you don't REALLY overcome the loss of business from obsolete products. At the best, you take some orders and ship some products. At least we are better than that. We realize when a business is a fake one. We can't live from a virtual business, can we?"

"Bingo." I am so happy to have Eliza around this table. I take it from there.

"I would like to propose a new sequence for product launches from now on. The assumption is that the first customer installation is in a way the bottleneck of the whole process. So I want to subordinate all other processes to it. Sound familiar?"

"You're bringing us several years back to when we first read 'The Goal.'" John is becoming nostalgic. This is the time for me to proceed.

"I'm basically proposing to protect our own people! When engineering presents a timetable for a new product, they really believe in it! They do that based on fifteen to twenty-five years of experience in new product development. However, and whatever method they use, they are more often wrong than right. They should not be blamed for that. It is all simply a matter of managing uncertainties. When you identify the constraint of a process, and when you subordinate all other processes to that constraint, you basically do exactly that – manage uncertainties."

"Roger, let's get to the bottom line; what's the new launch sequence that you propose." Gary is ever eager to come to a workable conclusion.

"Yes Gary, here it is:

(1) First customer installation: wait 30 to 60 days and move to the next step only if the product does some actual production;

(2) Official announcement: announce that the new product is available in six months at a higher price than the current offering;

(3) Beta sites: at least three. Focus on customer acceptance; do not recognize revenues on shipments until you have all three acceptances. This will put the whole focus on the acceptance process, and not on order taking or on revenues;

(4) Full customer availability or FCA.

Bottom line, the entire process is managed by real actions in the field, and not by a theoretical and usually unreliable time schedule."

"Roger, do you think we can take a corrective action with the Lilly." Eliza, who initiated the meeting, is now back in control.

"Yes, Eliza. Definitely. Here's how it will work. I will refrain from taking more orders for the Lilly. You will stop recognizing revenues for shipments of the Lilly. We will re-launch the product from Step 3: Get Customer Acceptance, at least three of them. Nothing will happen until then. Once we have the product working, we will implement the necessary changes on all other installed systems. When you tell us that customers are starting to pay, we will resume FCA, I mean Full Customer Availability."

"Roger, you must be nuts. You are the first VP of Sales that has ever proposed to refrain from order taking. The competition will kill you; I mean us. Do it all in parallel: make the product working, but continue to sell. Sell, sell, and sell. That's how money is being made." Pierce is at his best. Sell, sell, sell has always been his slogan.

"No, Pierce, Roger is right. We have to remember the goal – making money. Sales, market share, product shipments or revenues are not the goal. Shipping unreliable products is a generator of costs, not of cash. It is like ignoring a bottleneck. It is like making a non-bottleneck resource produce at its highest efficiency. So what? We've seen that movie too often. Roger, your proposal is accepted. Decision made!" Sometimes, I just love Gary. He is the best!

*   *   *

Pierce is visibly annoyed when we all leave the conference room. In fact, I do not recall if Gary has ever shut him down in public like he just did. This may not be that good for me, either. I know that Pierce and Ray talk. It's strange, but sometimes I feel like after every success, I am worse off politically. It should be the opposite, shouldn't it? Just when I arrive at my office, Amy calls me. Apparently, Pierce wants to have a follow-up discussion with Eliza and me in Gary's office. What the hell does he want? Didn't he have enough already?

Pierce is first to talk when all four of us are in the office. "We are making a strategic mistake, and I want to do whatever we can to avoid this."

"What do you mean?" Gary asks what seems to be an obvious question.

"Our company has always been built on growth. We need to grow, grow, and grow. That's what the shareholders are expecting from us, and that's what the analysts talk to us about all the time. Without double-digit growth, year in, year out, we will soon become a less interesting company and we will lose market share. We need to fix the problems with the Lilly while running. We cannot afford to hold back sales of scanners that represent over fifteen percent of our product portfolio."

"Eliza and Roger, what do you think?" This is very strange. While Gary was obviously annoyed in the large forum meeting, it seems that he is having a good time now. It is as if he is amused. Luckily, Eliza speaks first.

"Growth is indeed important, but growth is an outcome of actions. Forcing growth or a rate of growth very often leads to bad management."

"Roger?" Gary will not let me run away from this one.

"I agree with Eliza, I am afraid." I try to be gentle. "There is an important nuance here. It is like dealing with competition: some say that we need to develop products that can beat the competition. I always say that we have to first develop products that will meet real market needs when they are ready, and only then look at competition and make an assessment on positioning, and hence, resulting market share. This sounds like a nuance, but it's an important one.

"Or," Eliza interjects, "it's like pricing. I always say that we first need to look at market pricing and only then look at our costs and the gross margin, not the other way around. This order of thoughts may sound like an insignificant nuance, too, but it's a pretty important one. We first need to focus on our business, our products, our operations and the market. Then growth will follow."

I basically agree with Eliza—growth is an outcome. It's the result of our actions, not its cause. It's great when it comes, but it can be catastrophic when it is enforced, when there are no real foundations behind the growth. When there are no foundations, growth does not create value, it creates a bubble. And bubbles, we already know, tend to burst. Sooner or later."

"Pierce?" Gary really seems to enjoy this. I have never seen him like this before.

"Guys, guys, guys. My dear colleagues. We are all either shareholders, or at the minimum, options holders of this company. You sound to me as if you don't like money. This is how it works: if there's no growth in revenues, there's no growth in cash flow. If there's no growth in cash flow, there's no attractive company valuation. If there's no attractive valuation, there's low share price. If there's low share price, there's no money for the company shareholders. And definitely nothing for the option holders. And believe me, no money for the shareholders equals a new management for CGS. This is all up to you now."

"Pierce, my experience says otherwise." Gary talks to Pierce like a father talks to his son. "Bursting bubbles, like the one that Roger outlined, is what leads to new management. We need to be growth driven and to plan for it. However, growth is the result of real, tangible actions, which in turn stem from good planning. If we fail to plan well, or fail to execute the planning well, it is better to pay the price of the short-term consequences and regroup. Under my watch, our business will be real and healthy.

Eliza is definitely my partner for that, and she has all my respect and full back up as a CEO to a CFO. If we can't generate growth with good fundamentals, we won't. I believe that the fundamental improvements that the management team of CGS has managed in the last three quarters are real and warrant the gain in market share and our renewed growth. The Lilly is simply not ready. It was a disgrace to push it to the market, as it was used just to secure some artificial growth. I approved of it, and it was a mistake. I'm sorry I did it, and I will not be a party to it anymore."

I think that Pierce got what he deserved. He was defeated twice today – in public. However, I am not sure if we convinced him. For too many executives in our industry, growth has become a religion. This religion has often driven unworthy acquisitions and business malpractice. One of the reasons I've stayed at CGS for this long is because of Gary's solid attitude on the fundamentals of the business. I will never forget the lessons learned from him, and also from Eliza, on that topic.

Chapter 6
Multitasked Sales Support

August 16, Year 2

The day after this meeting I head quickly to the Courtyard Hotel on the Middlesex Turnpike. Chuck has gathered all our sales support staff from around the country for a three-day seminar. Chuck is really good at this. He brings a combination of presentation, games, group discussions and case studies with him. He always finds a multitude of ways to brainwash our guys.

Chuck and I said that we would hold a 30-minute discussion on why some of my sales people, mostly the remote ones, complain about the same 'black hole' effect in CGS's support that our Toronto rep complained about. Apparently, this is more of a common problem than I thought. I start by presenting the problem. "There are almost thirty people in this conference room. I'd like to hear at least five opinions why we as a group are not as responsive as we should be. Don't take this the wrong way. I am not at all interested in finger-pointing. I am solely driven by a desire to improve—fixing whatever needs to be fixed. I expect honest answers." I see that someone hesitantly raises his hand at the back of the room. I ask him to speak up.

"I am always dealing with multiple projects at the same time. Sometimes, I don't have the answers to all the problems or issues that arise, and I need to send a request for help from Engineering or from some of my colleagues who know more about certain topics than I do. While I send the request for some clarifications for one project, I start working on another one. Sometimes I wait too long for an answer, and sometimes the other project carries me away. The bottom line is that the answer is slow in coming." This makes sense to me. I see other hands in the air. I choose another person.

"Sometimes we need to refer back to the customers, too, for some clarifications, such as what computer platforms they use, or which attributes they use for a certain application. We cannot proceed without this information. Then it takes them forever until they respond. They, too, have black holes on their side."

"Some of the sales people expect a daily update on the progress of their project. When we tell them that it will take a week, they send us emails or voicemails two days later. I don't feel a need to reply to those, as there is nothing new to say. After all, a week is a week. And then we are blamed for being a black hole."

That was our third speaker. After few more such comments, they start repeating themselves. I think that I get the picture. Luckily, I have become a TOC expert myself. Well, not exactly an expert yet. But I was able to grasp some basic ideas. I can easily detect that we have a bad multitasking issue at hand. I decide to make a drawing on the board.

A	B	C	A	B	C	A	B	C	A	B	C

TIME

"Let's say you have three projects to work on: project A, project B and project C. You are all proudly working in multitasking mode: you start working on A, but then there is an Engineering issue, so you move to B; but then the Sales guy of C calls you, and under pressure by that guy, you really want to show some improvement, so you move to C. Then there is a customer specs issue, so you move back to A; and so on and so forth. We call that bad multitasking."

"Why?" Chuck is first to ask, "it's certainly multitasking, but why is it bad? You don't expect me to just sit around, doing nothing, waiting for the answer to come at project A? Instead of being idle, I help to advance both projects B and C. What's wrong with that?" He is visibly annoyed. He continues: "I have always been very proud to be a multi-tasking type of person! And CGS has invested a lot in us to make us such."

"Chuck, look at the drawing on the board and tell me when projects A, B and C would be completed. Assume that every box represents a week." Chuck counts quickly and responds:

"Project A is done after ten weeks, project B is done after eleven weeks and project C is completed after twelve weeks."

"Exactly. And how many weeks are in a quarter?"

"Approximately thirteen weeks"

"Right, how does it look with the three projects if I started them on week three of the quarter?"

He quickly counts, hesitates a little, and slowly answers: "In that particular instance it doesn't look good. You wouldn't have enough time to close anything by the end of the quarter." But he doesn't look convinced.

I continue: "Exactly." Now, I make another drawing on the board.

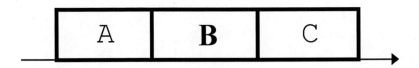

I ask Chuck what he sees. He looks at it, and then answers: "Roger, I see what you mean. Here, there is no multitasking and project A is ready after four weeks and project B is completed after eight weeks. So they may be ready soon enough to enable the closure of a deal even within the same quarter. However, you completely ignore what everyone said here—the need to bring some more information from other sources: either Engineering; or my colleagues; or the customers themselves. Such things prevent you from finishing your tasks, no matter what you do. It's a fact of life in our projects, and some of it is simply unavoidable."

"You are absolutely right. Let me make a third drawing."

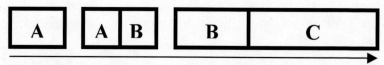

"Now, Chuck, what do we see? Or maybe someone else?" I point to the man who said that he was always working on multiple projects.

"I see what you mean, Roger. In the gaps in projects A and B, we are waiting for some answers from another source. We are idle for quite a long time. And yet projects A and B are completed in 5 and 10 weeks respectively, still earlier than weeks 10 and 11, when we did it all in a multitasking mode."

Chuck is still in fighting mode: "What do you expect us to do during the gaps, Roger? Go to the beach? Fly to Vegas?"

"Well, Chuck, if what I hear is correct, Vegas isn't a bad choice at this time of the year. You can get some great deals." I'm trying to lighten the tense atmosphere. "Not at all; focus on your current project, expedite the replies from your other sources, provide feedback on your current project to the relevant sales people, learn about a new product. Just do not do one thing – don't work on additional projects."

"But Roger, look at what happened to project C? It is now completed after 14 weeks instead of 12."

"Listen to me carefully." I look at the whole audience. I feel that I have their full attention: "What we did here is an oversimplification. I think that I would be correct in stating that you all deal with at least ten projects at one time. My problem, or rather our problem, is that all those projects take too long to be completed. In fact, if you are really functioning in complete multitasking mode, the amount of time you're spending on each project is the same amount of time that's actually needed to complete all ten! It takes ten times more than it should!

How many times have you heard our sales people say to you, 'I don't get it! Preparing a solution or a configuration should take not more than ten days. How come it takes you seven weeks? What the hell are you doing?'" I hear big laughs in the crowd. They all hear this constantly.

I proceed: "What I'm asking from all of you, with the help of Chuck, is to find a reasonable number of projects to do at the same time. Not ten and not one, but perhaps two or three. Focus on those; bring them to completion even if sometimes it seems that you have some idle time. Once you've decided on the number of projects you can comfortably deal with, don't exceed it! Don't be tempted to jump to another project, because then, for sure, you will lose focus.

"Only when you complete a project, I repeat, only then, should you take another one on. While you work on a project, make sure to provide ongoing feedback to the sales person, or to the reseller who wants to push the sales cycle of that project forward, or to the client. Responsiveness and on-time completion of projects are as important as the quality or the content of the projects themselves."

I pause to hear some feedback. Most of them nod when I look at them. I don't know if what we did was effective, but Chuck will surely monitor this closely as we move forward. I say a few more words; I tell everyone how important their contribution is, and how much I need them in the next coming weeks and months. I leave them in the capable hands of Chuck, and drive back to Crosby Drive, to my office.

*   *   *

When I arrive, I meet Gary in the corridor. He wants to talk to me. We both step into my office. Gary sits in front of me, and says in a somber tone; "Ray and Pierce have brought to my attention that you don't want Pierce to be involved in Sales any longer. One of the reasons we kept him around is because we wanted to continue capitalizing on his relationships. I think that you are giving up on that asset too easily. I must say that I am surprised and disappointed."

I can only imagine how Pierce and Ray presented their case. It looks like they are digging my grave in case I fail in one way or another. And they leave nothing to chance. What a nice work environment!

"Gary," I respond, "I simply asked Pierce to be active in a coordinated manner. He's jumping all around, bypassing me and my people. I'm trying to bring change to our mode of operation. For us not to just rely on traditional salesmanship, which is certainly important, but also a methodical approach to yield higher efficiencies in a complex and large sales organization. As I told you, it is my belief that we need to combine both worlds effectively. Relying solely on the traditional salesmanship that Pierce excels in causes us to rely too heavily on luck and chance, and we can no longer afford it. We can't depend on luck!"

"Gary, simply put, I am really trying to implement a new methodology in sales management. I think I have shown significant success in a very short amount of time. Pierce wants to force me back to his methods, and while I think that both of our methods complement each other, I have no intention whatsoever in giving up on mine."

"Roger, you have to be sensitive to Ray and Pierce. I am not telling you what to do; I'm just asking you to find a way to involve Pierce in sales. Don't give up on your new methods. I am not just asking, I'm practically begging that you do this."

"I'll do my best Gary." What else can I say?

*   *   *

Chuck comes in to see me late in the evening, after nearly everybody is gone. He starts by saying that I had a hell of a good 'show' at the Courtyard in front of all the sales support people. I realize that he is trying to overcome the fallout from our last meeting. After I take the compliment, I ask him what is going on. He obviously did not come just to tell me how good I am.

"Well, Roger, what you proposed sounds great. But it is all easier said than done! In order to stop multitasking, they basically have to say 'no' to some important projects, or at least to put them on hold. Now, they are kind of unofficially measured on the service that they provide to the sales guys. 'No' is not something you say easily to your customer."

"But Chuck, all of this started because their customers weren't happy. No? Remember the 'black hole' and all that stuff?'"

"You're right. But at least when they were working a little bit on a multitude of projects, they were showing advance here and there, and they didn't have to say 'no' to any requests."

"Yes, but the final outcome was still that they never completed any project on time. Or did they?"

"Don't get me wrong, Roger, your presentation made a lot of sense. I just don't see how it can be implemented that easily."

"I see. You know what; let me propose something to you. We have all the sales cycles entered into our system. You know the ten steps, don't you?"

"Of course I do."

"Good. My guess is that there is a well-defined, or at least easy-to-estimate time frame between step 4 – Letter of Understanding, and step 6 – Solution Proposal and Technical Check. Ask Chris to have a report of all step 4's submitted to you every day by email. The system can also send you the letters themselves, which will allow you to estimate what the scope of the specific project is. This is a kind of advance notice.

For the bigger projects, or more complicated ones, make sure that there is a sales support person available to take the hot potato when step 5 is completed. When they do that, don't let them work on anything else until the hot potato is moved to step 7 – Production Demo. Simply don't let them," I repeat.

"For those projects that are not too big or not too complex, and for which you don't have resources readily available, first try alternatives such as yourself; some knowledgeable service person; or even someone from Engineering. If no solution is found, then be proactive, and update the relevant sales person upfront that his project will be in a queue. He won't like it one bit, but it's much better than to keep him in the dark. At least you will not receive a daily complaint about the advancement of his project. Don't you think this might help?"

"Yes, it might." After a thought, he adds: " Why didn't I think about taking all step 4's from the system? This is the drum that sets the pace for all our work. I feel like an idiot now."

"Don't, Chuck. I must admit that I didn't invent the idea; I simply passed it on to you. I think that there is even a name for that in TOC. I believe that they call this the Resource Buffer. Anyway, it doesn't matter now. Do you think this will work? It's really important, you know."

"I know, and I am sure it'll work out one hundred percent. It's a pleasure working with you, Roger."

"Thanks, Chuck. Much appreciated."

I come home to find Joanna reading a book on the sofa in our living room. Joanna is always calm and in control. They say opposites attract. That's probably true, but I sometimes wish my own life would be less hectic. We sit together as Joanna prepares some coffee and we both talk about what we've been doing all day. I update Joanna about my discussions with Pierce and Gary. She listens carefully. Joanna is a great listener and an even greater thinker. I think that this is why I fell in love with her to begin with. Of course, she is as beautiful today as she was twenty years ago. Sometimes, I think that as a mature woman, she is more beautiful than ever.

After awhile she looks at me and says: "Honey, take the initiative, as always. Surprise Pierce; call on him to help you. After all, he has built all of those important relationships. You know that I'm not the sales expert, but I figure that what matters in the end is the number of sales. If that's the case, you need to make sure all resources are supporting your goals. Even if their name is Pierce."

"Jo, you're starting to sound like my boss. This is getting scary. Nonetheless, I'm afraid you might be right. That's exactly what Gary expects me to do. I need to be on the offensive again. Right now, they have all put me on the defensive, and all for internal political reasons. I wish I could focus only on the external fights."

"Roger, you are not that naïve, are you?"

"No, I've been a corporate beast for much too long. I am not that naïve."

We quickly change the subject. I know that Joanna is right. As usual, the evening's discussion in my own, personal and quiet environment helps me think in a much clearer way. This is something I can't do in the office at all.

*   *   *

Chapter 7
End-of-Quarter Syndrome

September 22, Year 2

Our sales are progressing. It isn't easy, it takes all my time, but it moves forward. It seems that some of the problem solving we have done is really turning into improvements. Sales are up for the third consecutive quarter now. It even seems that our post-sale operations are smoother too.

This Saturday, at nine A.M., I'm taking Lizzie to her soccer game. Her team is called the Omegas. Why? Well, they originally wanted to be called the Alphas, but some other team had already grabbed the first letter of the Greek alphabet. Beta didn't sound cool, so they decided to take the first letter, but from the other end of the alphabet. So they are called the Omegas. She has really become good at soccer.

We both wake up early. We eat a quick breakfast. Joanna and Jennifer are still asleep. It's a beautiful day outside. Lizzie has asked the coach to let her play offense in this game. She really wants to score another goal before the end of this season. She's all excited, and looks great wearing the Omega team's red shirt.

We are in the fourth quarter of the game; the score is still zero to zero. The kids are running around like crazy on the field. A guy who is standing next to me is a parent of another girl on the Omega team.

He mumbles: "If they would only put as much effort in the whole game as they're doing now in the fourth quarter, they would win for sure."

"What do you mean?" I ask him. "How do you know they would win?"

"I have been a coach for the last five years, but I'm getting too old for it now. In the game it's always the same; at the beginning, they play slowly just to see how the other team is doing. They want to get a feel for who is who on the other team. It is only towards the end, if they are either losing or if there is a tie that they start pushing like crazy. It would have all been very different if they had pushed like that from the very first minute of the game."

"So, did you come up with a solution?"

"No" he responds, but before he continues, I hear shouts from all over. The Omegas have scored. I haven't seen it, but I join the shouting too. Lizzie runs towards me and gives me a hug. I am so proud of her. This is a good start to the weekend. The Omegas have won. Red rules! Yeaaaahhhhh!

On the way back, I think about what that other guy said. It reminds me of the student syndrome in project management. Students ask for as much time as possible before an exam, but then they start learning at the very last minute. The same happens in a project: task managers ask for as much time as possible, and by that they introduce as much safety as possible, but at the end, all or most of it is. How do we know? Well, the projects so rarely end on time. So why does it bother me now? How is this related to what I do? For some reason I can't make the link.

Lizzie and I get home. It's almost noon already. Joanna has prepared some lunch. We eat it outside on the porch. An hour later, with a coffee in our hands, Joanna asks:

"Lizzie came back from the game really happy. She said she is the one who passed the ball to the girl who scored."

"Yes, she did. It was a great pass." There is no way I'm going to tell her that I didn't see it because I was chatting with one of the fathers. "She did great."

"Great." After a while, she asks: "Will you be very busy next week? I'd like you to come home early for once. I need some time to complete a big project."

"Joanna, how can you ask that now? You know that this is the last week of the quarter. The pressure will be unbearable as usual; I will need to be at ten different locations at once. I will be on the phone non-stop."

"Tell me, smart guy, how come you don't work that hard the whole quarter? Why do you all wait for the very, very last minute to close deals?"

I almost spit out my coffee as it dawns on me: it's just like in the soccer game; it's just like in the student syndrome. At the end there is never enough time to finish the job. How come? Why is all the effort made at the last minute? Why is it that all the safety, quite often sizable, doesn't help at the end? And why can't we take as many orders in the first week of the quarter as in the last one? We all know that the pressure to close and the uncertainty of the outcome when approaching the last days of the quarter are killing us psychologically. This disrupts the whole operation and often makes all our forecasting pointless.

"You know" I say to Joanna, "I think I'll be able to come home early on Thursday." The next thing I do is make a phone call to Barry.

"Barry, this is Roger, I'm sorry to disturb you during the weekend."

"That's okay Roger. How can I help you?"

"Barry, in the same way that TOC helped to overcome the student syndrome in project management, I would like it to help me solve the end-of-quarter-syndrome in sales. I would like you to spend the last week of the quarter with me. You'll see, it's the highest-pressure week in the quarter and it looks like a war room. Then, during the next quarter, I want you to help us solve this syndrome, once and for all."

"No problem, Roger, I'll have to shift some meetings on Monday and Tuesday, but I believe I'll be able to meet with you most of the time this week and the week after. This doesn't mean we'll find a solution to your problem that fast, but at least we should know where we stand by then."

*　　*　　*

After some early office meetings, I make some phone calls to my staff to test the water. Well, it's at the boiling point. Nothing unusual. Our quarter proceeds more or less the same. As usual, we depend on some big deals that can make or break the quarter. And, of course, the deals all close at the very last minute. After some thoughts, I stand up and go to Pierce's office. I know he's in today. When he sees me, he doesn't flash his trademark smile.

I don't smile either. I get straight to the point. "Pierce, I need your help. There is a four million dollar deal on the table. The customer is American Publishing. As you know very well, they are the largest magazine publishing house in the country. They have decided to do a major upgrade to their facility. In fact, we're talking about multiple facilities here. They want to be able to localize, to produce local versions of their magazines across the country. To achieve it, they need to transmit the common portions of their magazines in a fast and economic manner. Then they want to add the local content and print locally. I think that they like our solution a lot, but we are something like thirty percent more expensive than our competitor. So far, I have not agreed to reduce our offer."

"Roger, are you feeling okay? Are you aware of what you're asking me to do? Not too long ago, you made a full-blown scandal out of a few meetings between me and some remote customers, and now you want me in on the largest deal in the quarter?"

"Pierce, as you said it yourself, we are both stakeholders in this company. We need to make the best out of it. You know Jim Angle, the owner-chairman of American Publishing. He listens to you. He trusts you. We need that deal badly. We need it now. I am asking you to get involved."

"Does Gary know about it? Did he ask you to get me involved?"

"No, no. I 've done this on my own initiative."

"I see." He thinks for a moment and adds, "I may need to give in on the price somehow."

"Pierce, let's bring the local sales person and his district management on the line. We can strategize together. I am willing to discount our offer, but only if I know there is a point. I don't want to sell us short. I really believe that our solution is what they truly need."

"Bring them on the line. I know Jim Angle very well. We've played golf together in one of the nicest resorts in the world. It was lots of fun. I have his phone number at home. I can call him during the weekend."

"Pierce, this weekend is too late; we need this now," I say, decisively.

"No problem, Roger, I can call him now".

"Great." If Joanna were here, I would give her a big kiss. She is so smart. What would I ever do without her?

Barry has his own way to deal with complex issues. He convinced me that the best way to solve such problems as the end-of-quarter syndrome is to bring together a group of people who have had experience dealing with the problem. We first need to be able to verbalize the problem in more detail. Then we need to find its root cause, or causes. Only then, when we agree on the source of our problems, can we develop a possible solution.

As I was planning to visit our Santa Ana office anyway, Barry and I take the morning flight to California. After a bumpy landing at the John Wayne Airport in Orange County, we go to the hotel. We refresh ourselves and then head to a meeting with all our sales staff in Southern California. We have a District Sales Manager here who manages eight sales people. All nine of them are already in the conference room when Barry and I enter.

Joe, the Sales Manager, starts the meeting. "We are honored to host our VP here, Roger Mirton, as well as Barry Kahn who is a consultant to Gary Calleso, our CEO. Roger asked me to bring a bunch of brains together to solve an important problem that affects the whole company, not just Southern California. So here we are, we'll give it our best shot. Roger, they are all yours."

"Thanks, Joe. It's a pleasure to see you all. Barry and I would like to hold a discussion here on what we call the end-of-quarter syndrome. As you all know, the proportion of orders that come in on the last days of the quarter is always bigger than in any other period during the quarter. This creates a huge load on all the parts of the company, from Engineering to Production to Installation, and so on. We would like to hear your views and opinions as to why this is the case.

"Instead of having all of us jumping in and providing a wide variety of answers and opinions, we have prepared a set of questions here that we would like to ask you. Please feel free with your answers. This is not a test of any kind. We want the real input from the field." They are looking at me. There is some skepticism in the air. They don't say a word.

I continue: "Let me start by asking the first question: What are the main problems or issues that are, in your opinion, the main cause of taking more orders late in the quarter rather than early?"

"Pressure from you people, in corporate management," one of the guys at the back shoots first. I don't know what his name is.

"Okay, let me write that down. If you don't mind, I'll number the problems. Let's number that 100: Corporate is putting more pressure on Sales toward the end of the quarter. Now, I need some more."

"Discounts." This is Laura. She is the only woman in the room.

"What do you mean, Laura?"

"Well, customers know that we'll give them bigger discounts when we are under pressure. They know very well that we are all under pressure to close deals towards the end of the quarter. So they wait till the last minute to get a bigger discount."

"I see. There are quite a few issues you are pointing to here." I write on the board: First issue is: 110. CGS is known to give higher discounts when under pressure, and then: 120. CGS is always under high pressure to close quarter with as many sales as possible, and also: 130. Customers are aware of the pressure at the end of the quarter and lastly 135. Customers wait till the last minute to get better terms from CGS. "Okay, give me more."

Joe decides that he must add his managerial perspective: "Quarterly financial measurement. The quarterly reports are the invention of the accountants. We don't need to be measured that way."

"Good point." 140. CGS is measured by the financial community on a quarterly basis."

We continue that way, and before long, we have the following statements on the board:

> 100. Corporate is putting more pressure on Sales toward the end of the quarter.
>
> 110. CGS is known to give higher discounts when under pressure.
>
> 120. CGS is always under high pressure to close quarter with as many sales as possible.
>
> 130. Customers are aware of the company's pressure at the end of the quarter.
>
> 135. Customers wait until the last minute to get better terms from CGS.
>
> 140. The financial community measures CGS on a quarterly basis.
>
> 150. There is a growing pressure to deliver equipment at the very end of the quarter.
>
> 160. Customers order our equipment for the short term.
>
> 170. All incentive plans are quarterly based.
>
> 180. The backlog of CGS is not increasing.
>
> 190. There is no clear definition of delivery times.
>
> 200. CGS will sometimes deliver even when an order is submitted in the last week of the quarter.
>
> 210. Most our orders come at the end of the quarter.

"Okay," I continue from here, "we have enough issues for now. Please help us to find cause-and-effect connections among these statements."

"What do you mean by that?" somebody asks.

I try to answer: "For example: If 'CGS is known to give higher discounts when under pressure,' and if 'customers are aware of the company's pressure at the end of the quarter,' then 'customers wait until the last minute to get better terms from CGS.' Does that make sense?" They all nod. It really makes sense. Common sense!

"I have another one," says Laura. I am happy that everyone is participating. "Here it goes: if 'the financial community measures CGS on a quarterly basis,' and if 'the backlog of CGS is not increasing,' then 'CGS is under higher pressure to close the quarter with as many sales as possible.' How about that Roger?"

"That's great, Laura. Anybody else?"

"I have one, too." Joe needs to show that he is the boss, doesn't he?

"Yes, Joe, go ahead."

"Mine is as follows: if 'all incentive plans are quarterly based' and if 'corporate is putting more pressure on Sales toward the end of the quarter,' then 'most orders (indeed) come at the end of the quarter.'"

"Joe, let me see if I understand. You are implying here that sales people will work harder at the end of the quarter because of their incentives, and because of the pressure from corporate. What you're saying is that hard work at the end of the quarter will actually lead to more orders coming at the end of the quarter?"

"Yes, Roger, that is exactly what I meant."

"So let me add that: '220. Sales people work much harder to close deals at the end of the quarter.' I'll take all your statements, as well as the connections among them, as you've pointed out, and put it all in one single scheme. This scheme describes the cause-and-effect relationships among your many problems. We call it Current Reality Tree, or CRT for short.

Let's write your statements on some sticky notes, and then arrange them in a way that makes sense. The arrows between statements are used as follows: '*If* the bottom of the arrow exists, *then* the head of the arrow must happen.'" We work together for about half an hour, and before long, we have the following kind of awkward structure:

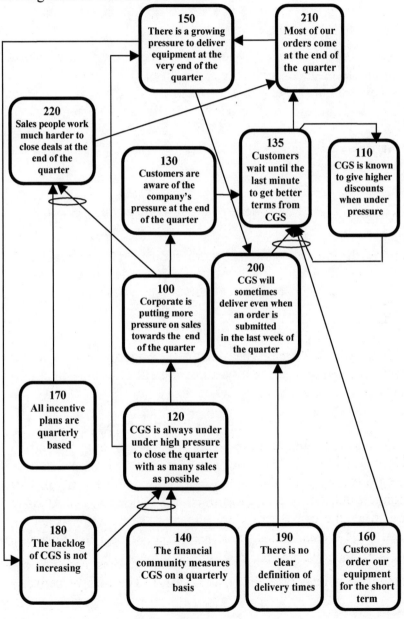

It isn't so easy to create such a structure. I feel it's about time to get some professional help. I ask Barry to intervene and comment on our Current Reality Tree. He followed the entire process without as much as one word. He just jotted some notes. I think this is the first time I've seen a consultant who can keep his mouth shut. He is really something.

"You have all done a wonderful job. According to your analysis, all the problems, which we refer to in TOC lingo as UDE's, or UnDesirable Effects, are interconnected. They all stem from few basic causes. You are pointing to five fundamental reasons for late orders in the quarter. But as I see it from my perspective, there may be fewer than that. So what do we have at the bottom of our CRT?

140.   The financial community measures CGS on a quarterly basis.

160.   Customers order equipment for the short term.
170.   All incentive plans are quarterly based.
180.   The backlog of CGS is not increasing.
190.   There is no clear definition of delivery times.

But we are also seeing many recursive patterns here, or loops; i.e. cause and effect relationships that interact and strengthen each other. This is a strong indication of how powerful the trend is, or how difficult it is to overcome. Let us see, for example: the relationship between statements 135 and 110 is the following: the more you are known to give better terms late in the quarter, the more customers will wait. And the more they will wait while the external pressure remains, the more you will give better terms. This is a dangerous and vicious cycle. Also, as much as the backlog does not increase, the pressure to deliver more and recognize revenues increases, but then the more you deliver, the lower the backlog is."

"Barry," I interrupt, "what is involved, in your view, with the issue of delivery times and recognition?"

"Yes, that's a good question. Let's take an extreme case. If CGS had a strict policy of one month delivery, no matter what, the end of the quarter pressure wouldn't help us because, as we all know, the pressure is on revenues, and orders become recognized by our financial system as revenues only when equipment is delivered. If revenues weren't created because of the strict delivery terms, then added pressure at the end of the quarter wouldn't help revenues. Also, customers would know that they should not wait until the last minute to place their orders."

"Barry, this is all true, but customers tend to order equipment after they have been informed that they have won a large bid. And then, they are under a huge pressure to get that equipment quickly, which makes our delivery times a competitive advantage."

"This is it, Roger. Strict delivery times bring rigidity to the system. In business, flexibility is often the thing that creates your advantage relative to your competition. Furthermore, even if it were implemented, it would, at best, advance the syndrome by a month. This not what we are trying to achieve, is it? What is needed now is to see whether or not we can eliminate some of the root causes, so that their disastrous consequences are prevented.

Let's see what else we have:

140. The financial community measures CGS on a quarterly basis. This is a fact-of-life. As long as Wall Street does it, we won't be able to change it, no matter what. CGS's financial people simply convey it to you. We'll need to find a way to deal with it.

160. Customers order equipment for the short term. This is another fact of life. As you said, customers do not take the risk of

buying equipment when they do not have the business to justify it. Once they do, they need the equipment ASAP. There is nothing we can do to change that paradigm.

190. There is no clear definition of delivery times. As mentioned before, strict delivery times of, say, one month would merely change the end-of-quarter syndrome to end-of-last-day-to-recognize-revenues-this-month syndrome. Also, flexible delivery times are a competitive advantage of CGS; let's not ruin it.

180. The backlog of CGS is not increasing. This is not an operational issue. It's an unfortunate result of our inability to sell more. You have to find a way to increase order taking so that a backlog can be maintained and increased. But, let's put that aside as well for the time being.

170. All incentive plans are quarterly based. This is a paradigm that has existed forever in this company, as well as in others. However, it isn't one of the Ten Commandments, and I think the time has come to challenge it. What I propose, Roger, is that we do this off-line and that we 'release our hostages' for now."

"You are absolutely right, Barry." I thank Joe, Laura and all the other sales people in our Southern Californian team for their input. We have a short break and then review some large orders that are in the make. We continue to chat for a short while, and then say goodbye to all.

That same evening, Joe and I have dinner with our biggest customer in California. There is a $3.2 million deal on the table, with lots of equipment. I do my best to help my staff, and myself, obviously. It is funny to see that delivery time is emphasized again. They are after a government bid. If they win, they are committed to almost immediate deliveries, which means we need to supply the equipment almost overnight. If they lose the bid, they won't need the equipment at all. How can I explain that to the people in operations who always want a forecast three months in advance?

*   *   *

While Barry and I eat breakfast the next morning, we exchange some words about the results of our meeting yesterday. I think that it was really fruitful. After coffee, Barry points to the similarities between what we are encountering here, in Sales, and between what Engineering had faced prior to the implementation of TOC in project management. He suggests that we take a conference room at the business center in our hotel and bring Ron, our VP of Engineering, on the line for a conference call. I agree. My next meeting with one of Laura's customers is at 2:00 this afternoon, so we have plenty of time.

Barry goes to set it up. It actually works. "Ron, hi, this is Roger. I'm here with Barry. Listen, you have been deeply involved with TOC and it's been very successful for you, according to what Barry has told me. As I explained when we met last time, we are currently implementing TOC in Sales. We look at sales as a sequence of activities. There is a lot of uncertainty that each activity will finish on time. However, the interdependence between the activities in a certain sequence is very high. To me it looks very much like projects."

"Yes, Roger, this sounds very familiar."

"Now, we had to run a whole process here. Our goal is to bring sales in on time – whatever this means – but certainly don't want to rush it all in at the very end of the quarter. This, I think, is very similar to your R&D projects that were running quietly until someone realized that they would not finish on time, and from then on it all became a nightmare."

"Now, with TOC, you have mostly overcome that. I want to overcome that too. One last thing, Ron. It seems that the fundamental problem lies in our own policy to measure our sales force and provide incentives on a quarterly basis. I don't know how to change this process. Nevertheless, here we are. What do you say? Can you help us?"

"Roger, I understand you're dilemma and I think that maybe I can help you. The most difficult issue in implementing TOC in project management wasn't the introduction of a new computer system to plan, track and control the projects. No. The most difficult part was to move from one paradigm to another. Remember, in every project we had to remove the individual in-steps embedded safety in order to accumulate it all as buffer at the end of the project. For the sake of simplicity, I am ignoring other buffers for now, like what we call Feeding Buffers, or Resource Buffers. I am talking solely about the Project Buffer. The meaning of that is far-reaching for the performer of each task in a project.

"Imagine this scenario: 'Dear project task performer, we want you to assess the time it will take you to perform this task without the cushioning of any special built-in safety. We are okay with a fifty percent probability of completion on time.' And now comes the punch line: 'We want you to do your absolute best to complete the task on time, and we will monitor the process, but if you don't, it's okay too. After all, fifty percent probability of completion on time is also fifty percent probability of not on-time completion.'"

"Roger, can you imagine the change of mindset from an environment in which we literally punished the ones who did not meet deadlines, to an environment of understanding that phenomenon?"

"Do you mean that you are confirming that our quarterly measurement, and the incentive scheme of our own sales people is indeed the core of the problem?"

"Well, Roger, I don't know that for sure. What I am telling you 's that in our case, in Engineering, this was my biggest challenge. However, once that was overcome, the payoffs were huge. We now have an army of developers who give aggressive time possible for every task in the development process. That's why we call it ABP times – Aggressive, But Possible. What is funny is that they do their utmost to complete their task within this aggressive time.

"They know that we will understand if they are late – this will usually affect just the project buffer, not necessarily the end-date of the project. But they also know that we got rid of the student syndrome, which caused them to delay the start of an activity, and of the unnecessary perfectionism and creativity which caused them to consume the existing safety buffers when completing steps earlier than anticipated. Isn't that the greatest achievement of all?" It sounds a little complicated, but Ron is a man of long sentences.

Before I can fully understand his answer, Barry interjects: "Ron is right, Roger. The moment the shift is made, we have seen that many tasks, in spite of being assigned ABP times, are completed on time anyway. You move from a situation where all tasks' safety is systematically consumed whether a problem occurs or not, to a stage in which only few tasks eat the project buffer up. And here comes the solution to the big uncertainty factor. Very often, there is just one step of the project that can consume the entire project buffer, or most of it. Unfortunately, one never knows in advance which step this will be.

"Fortunately, in the new Critical Chain method, there is a project buffer that can absorb the result of that bad surprise, and the whole project can still be completed on time."

"Okay, Barry, I understand that, and now let's translate that all to my world of sales."

"Roger, from what I gather right now, the translation might be, well, revolutionary."

"Go on, Barry. After all I have been through since taking this job, I'm not easily scared off. Let's see where this leads."

"I hear you guys are doing very well on your own," says Ron.

"Sorry," I say to him, "it's simply that your remarks are very relevant to us."

"But we don't want to take any more of your time," adds Barry. "Thanks."

"Anytime, folks."

Barry and I go on with our issue. Barry continues: "Well, let's assume that your project is annual sales. You are committed to provide CGS with a given amount of sales within given twelve months."

"Well, it actually is."

"You have divided your project into four steps, four milestones—the famous quarters. You want each step to be on target. Your sales people are measured on that quarterly target. Their incentive plan is based on that target. So what do they do? They negotiate this target with you! The lower the target is, the better off they may turn out to be. This is exactly the same as a development engineer adding safety time to his project task. They negotiated that, too, prior to the implementation of the TOC project management."

"So? I still don't see the similarity."

"So, it might be quite similar. Change the words 'completion time' to 'dollar target' and buffer (in days) to buffer (in dollars). That's it. Agree with your guys on a target that they can meet in each step (i.e. each quarter) with fifty percent probability. Motivate them to achieve it, but obviously don't punish them if they don't. Whatever amount of dollars is not achieved in a certain quarter should be removed from the project buffer. Remember, the project is in terms of annual sales." It's still fuzzy to me.

"Barry, let's talk about a certain example."

"Okay, but before that, I will also propose to split the annual sales project into twelve months rather than in four quarters. You will see why later."

"Go on, Barry."

"Say that you want a sales person to close $4.8 million in business in a year. That means an average sale of $0.4 million per month. However, in dividing it into twelve monthly segments, point out to him that you want him to close $0.6 million per month! Of course, the chances for him doing that are low, say fifty percent, or even less. Still, say that this is your expectation, and reach an agreement with him or her that that's the monthly goal, and you will monitor it as such.

"However, failure to do so is not a failure! Even more, make sure he or she realizes that the incentives are not based on that. Remember the student syndrome. When targets are low, or well negotiated by sales, there is no need to hurry in the first days; everything can be delayed to the last minute. Also, when there is a lot of time, every deal is negotiated more than necessary, exactly like every software code is reviewed and brought to perfection unnecessarily. Now, with a large, to some even an unrealistic target, one has to run, run, and run."

For some reason it reminds me of a movie I recently watched called 'Run, Lola, Run.' Well, it's a lot of running. I try to understand.

"If our sales person actually runs and runs, sometimes successfully and sometimes unsuccessfully, what about the project buffer?"

"The project buffer consists of $2.4 million on the top annual sales target; the difference between the $7.2 million (12 x 0.6) and the $4.8 million you actually expect." When Barry sees my glazed eyes, he continues: "You see, let's say that the actual monthly sales for the first 4 months are (in million $'s): 0.1, 0.6, 0.4 and 0.4. As you can see, the first month was really difficult.

message to the poor sales guy at this stage should be constructive and helpful, not a punishment or a hit to his incentive plan. The project buffer, which was set at $2.4 million dives after the first month to $1.9 million. Why? Because he brought in sales of only hundred thousand – fully half a million less than expected.

"The next month he was on the target; he brought in $0.6 million. The buffer stays unchanged. If we look just at the buffer, at the end of each month respectively, what we see is (in million's): 1.9, 1.9, 1.7, and 1.5. The sales guy hits his buffer slowly. His mindset though remains focused on a $600,000 per month. He should be working pretty hard for that. The bonus comes with the completion of the project on target at the end of the project, i.e. $4.8 million at the end of the year. The bonus should be based on that!"

I try to digest what he just said. "Barry, I am stunned and amazed. This is so much different from all that I've seen throughout my entire career." On second thought I add: "It runs contrary to what we've always done with sales force motivation. Let me think about it for a minute." After another moment, I say: "It seems to be the right solution to our problem, but I have to scrutinize it carefully."

Then I think about it some more, and tell him: "Barry, I think we cracked this one, too."

"Roger, this is what makes my work so much fun. It will be even more exciting to implement it. Do you believe this can be done?" I think to myself for few seconds. It's a good question. Then, I answer:

"Yes, I do. We'll talk again very soon."

* * *

The first call I get in the morning is from Chuck. Not our Chuck, the one from Toronto. He sounds very annoyed: "Roger, you better have a word with your sales support guys. Since you and I last talked, we haven't seen much progress. The black hole is still there. What we've seen so far has not been very nice. We are getting some very blunt responses from your people lately. They tell us in a very direct manner that some of the things we are asking them to do won't be done. Or it will be done weeks from now. What's going on?" What can I say? After seeing that my effort to pacify him fails, I promise Chuck an answer later today, and call Chuck. Our own Chuck.

After many long-distance calls, the following picture emerges: after the sales support people meeting we had, the team in Canada decided on a "policy of truth" which means no more BSing the clients. "If there is something we can't do, we tell them directly. If it takes a lot of time, we don't tell them it's just a matter of days, we tell the truth. That's what management wants us to do, isn't it. And, by the way, they have never told the guys at *Imagine*, our Canadian partner, that they wouldn't do something. They simply gave truthful responses as per our guidelines. In other words, in order to avoid bad multi-tasking, they were refusing to take on more projects until completion of the ones they were handling. What happened next is not so positive: the Canadian guys from *Imagine* told our sales support staff that if their submitted requests would not get a reply in the form of a professional technical proposal within two weeks, such a reply would no longer be necessary. So, of course, our guys didn't give in to that pressure and told them to suit themselves."

A kindergarten, a regular kindergarten, that's what I'm running not a respected and successful sales organization. I try my best to improve our performance, and this is what I get! Once again I'm seeing the proof that the best way to arrive straight to hell is by following the road signs that say 'good intentions'. I have a long conference call with the Canadian team, and try peacefully to explain that the 'in your face' approach isn't what I meant.

There are many ways to say the 'truth', and theirs seems to be one of the more counter-productive ones. And when I mean 'truth', it doesn't mean we'll not make an utmost effort to reduce our response times. Not just say it, but actually do it. I hope I don't sound too threatening, but their quick (too quick) agreement to everything I say hints otherwise. Okay, this is really getting annoying. Then I call Chuck again. The one in Canada, and ask him to judge us on our performance, not on our politeness. Of course, I promise him that he won't ever hear again that we won't do something. We talk for about half an hour, and we end by setting a meeting in Toronto in two months. As if I don't have enough frequent flier miles already.

*　　*　　*

It's really funny how the stock market behaves. The moment our sales started to grow again, nothing happened. Now, after three consecutive quarters of growth, the confidence in CGS is finally coming back, and the share price is coming closer and closer to the $40 level. When I took over Sales, we had just plummeted from $45 to $18. We went even further down, to below $15. I hope that Ray, still a major company shareholder, remembers that I am part of this comeback.

Joanna and I have a late dinner in our kitchen.

"Jo, honey, I'd like to consult with you on something. Is your mind clear enough at this late hour or would you prefer to talk another time? It's about money."

"Go ahead, Roger. No problem."

"We have 15,000 options that will vest this Thursday – in three more days. The share price went up nicely. We could make a lot of money. But I don't know if we should exercise and take the money now, or wait. Perhaps the share price will continue to increase. There is a lot of money involved here."

"What is a lot of money?"

"The exercise price is $19. The share price is $40. If this remains unchanged until Thursday, we'll have (40–19) x 15,000 = $315,000. This does not include taxes of course, but let's leave that aside for now."

"Wow, that's a lot of money. Why not take it?"

"Jo, the share price is on an upward trend. It has been above $45 in the past already. I am in charge of Sales at CGS and I think that we can maintain the growth in our business, at least for a while longer. For the sake of our calculation, let's assume that the share price crosses $50, and then we exercise. The outcome, tax excluded, would be (50 – 19) x 15,000 = $465,000. This is a difference of $150,000. How can we possibly give that up?"

"Roger, I saw the little diagram that you made for your dad when he asked you to interfere with your sister's love life. It was quite successful. He backed off, and the next thing we saw she wasn't with this guy anymore. You said that this often helps you to solve conflicts in life, as well as on the job. Why don't we try this again here?"

"Yes, this may work here as well. Let's try. Let's see. The purpose is clear: make the Mirton family wealthier." After awhile I come up with a really simplistic chart. I can't believe this will be of any help this time. However, I draw it on a piece of paper that I find in the kitchen.

Joanna looks at it. I tell her that the trick is to find out whether or not each statement is a necessary condition to the one at its right. You can test it easily, if you add, between any two statements, the word REALLY. She says she wants to give it a try. When I try to help, she delicately declines it.

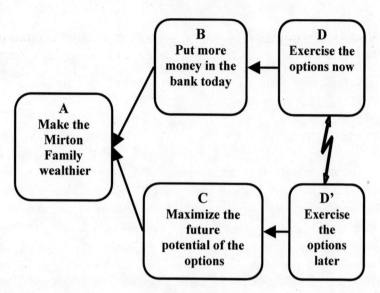

"I'll do it alone: 'In order for the Mirton family to become wealthier, it REALLY needs to put more money in the bank today.' Roger, this sounds bulletproof. There is nothing any of us can find against it. So let's proceed: 'In order to put more money in the bank today' we REALLY need to 'exercise now'. Sounds very convincing to me."

"Now let's move to the lower branch: 'In order to 'make the Mirton family wealthier,' we REALLY need to 'maximize the future potential of the options.' Well, so far it's okay. Let's continue. To 'maximize the future potential of the options,' we REALLY have to 'exercise later.'"

She stops to think. When I open my mouth to help her, she signals me to stay put. I'm smart enough to know when to shut up. Like now. Joanna continues:

"Roger, this completely stinks! How can anyone in this world know that the share price will go up in the foreseeable future?"

"You know very well how I think about the stock market. There is no logic behind it; at least none that I can grasp."

"So here it is. I think that we heard our banker once talk about the difference between investing and gambling. My summary is as follows. Waiting is gambling: taking the money now and investing it in a sound, diversified portfolio is investing. Please don't gamble with the Mirton's family money. Is that fair to say?"

I say to myself quietly "How can you be so stupid, Roger Mirton," and to Joanna I quickly reply: "Absolutely Jo. And you are right—waiting in hope for the additional $150K is too much of a gamble, and I hate gambling. We'll take the money this Thursday and we'll find a good way to invest it. I don't know if you helped me, or if you helped me to help myself. Anyway, thanks. I love you."

"I love you, too, Roger."

"And then," I add, "we'll be able to make good on our promise to donate some money to charity."

"Yes," she answers, "it's about time to make good on the $5,000 we promised to donate to the homeless shelter on State Street. Come to think of it, let me call Sue, she might want to join us this weekend for a visit at the shelter."

I answer: "Sure, that's a great idea, let's do it."

*   *   *

Gary and I get together for our weekly meeting. We call this a weekly meeting, but we're lucky if we hold this meeting once per month. But we don't change the name; we know too well that if it becomes a monthly meeting, we'll have only four or five of these a year. There are always excellent reasons for not having the meetings; we are either traveling or doing something else. Anyway, we speak often over the phone.

We review the business situation again. I need his help to close some big orders. In a way, both he and Pierce are kind of working for me now. I don't even mention the problem we have in Toronto. I simply hope that in a month or so it will be history. We also talk about some personnel issues. One of the District Sales Managers will be leaving soon for personal reasons. We need to find a replacement. After awhile Gary looks at me and says:

"Roger, you know that I'm going to retire towards the middle of next year, around summertime."

"Yes, you mentioned that to me awhile ago."

"Perhaps I shouldn't mention this now, but I think you should know that as for now, the preferred candidate to replace me – at least from the Board's point of view - is Pierce. He is the most experienced. He has the best track record." When Gary mentions the Board in this case, I am sure he's referring to Ray. Somehow, it seems, I have not been able to convince Ray that I've had a lot to do with the company turnaround in the last few quarters.

"Gary, to be frank, I prefer not to deal with this now. I am totally focused on doing my job and on succeeding. Also, since I trust you more than anyone else, I know that you will end up making the right recommendation to the Board. If you go with Pierce, I will understand. As you know, Pierce and I have a completely different style of management, but over all, we get along quite well now. I have a lot of respect for Pierce."

"I am very pleased by this response Roger. I was afraid that you would react differently, but after getting to know you, I'm really not surprised. Thank you."

"Thanks to you too Gary. Thank you for sharing that with me. I have to get going now. There is a lot on my plate."

*   *   *

I have gathered my four Regional Sales Managers in Bedford. I've asked Gary, Pierce and Eliza to join the meeting, too. Per my request, Eliza brought Nancy to the meeting as well. Nancy is our Director of Human Resources. I know a lot of people think that HR is just a waste of a company's money, that we could do all of HR's work with one clerk and a printer, especially since the work contracts are quite similar to each other and are easy to put together in most cases.

I have a different opinion; dealing with people requires a lot of experience. There are a lot of employee issues that HR assists me with, especially in times of trouble. So, I'm glad she's at this emergency meeting.

It amazes me that more than one year has passed since I took over Sales. I want to introduce my new incentive scheme for next year. At CGS, we always hold our annual sales kick-off meeting during the second week of January. At that time, towards the end of the meeting, we also hand over the incentive plans to each and every sales person. In order to do that, we need to have a very clear idea of what we expect every member of our sales force to do. If we can agree on the concept in October, we can finalize the details in November. We can do that in conjunction with the closure of the budget for next year.

I start the meeting by presenting the first run of our numbers for the next budget year. We have a BBS table. BBS stands for Backlog, Bookings, and Shipments. The term "shipments," in our case, is a synonym for revenues. Most people don't remember why we call this the BBS table. Anyhow, our BBS table for next year looks as follows.

[in million dollars]	Budget Year				
	Q1	Q2	Q3	Q4	Total
Beginning Backlog	40	42	72	55	40
Bookings	250	285	245	305	1,085
Revenues	248	255	262	270	1,035
End Backlog	42	72	55	90	90

I ask everyone to notice a few things. First, this is the first year we are targeting to go over a billion dollars. Wow! Second, while we anticipate that the bookings stream will fluctuate through the different seasons, we are planning for a steady three to four percent increase in revenues quarter by quarter. We can do this by taking more orders and managing the shipments in a sound manner. This is not rocket science. I point to the fact that our beginning of budget year backlog is not large. Indeed. Forty million dollars represents only fourteen days of backlog. This is very poor. Assuming the revenues target next year for Q1 will be around $278M, we are targeting a backlog of almost thirty days. Forty-five days is ideal, but we have to manage the improvement process gradually. As I want to make this all very tangible to everyone, I put the BBS for the four Regions + International on the screen, too. It looks like this:

[in million dollars]	Budget Year - Northwestern Region				
	Q1	Q2	Q3	Q4	Total
Beginning Backlog	7	9	15	15	7
Bookings	57	62	58	64	241
Revenues	55	56	58	60	229
End Backlog	9	15	15	19	19

[in million dollars]	Budget Year - Central Region				
	Q1	Q2	Q3	Q4	Total
Beginning Backlog	6	8	12	12	6
Bookings	37	40	37	38	152
Revenues	35	36	37	38	146
End Backlog	8	12	12	12	12

[in million dollars]	Budget Year - Southwestern Region				
	Q1	Q2	Q3	Q4	Total
Beginning Backlog	7	9	13	15	7
Bookings	57	60	60	64	241
Revenues	55	56	58	60	229
End Backlog	9	13	15	19	19

[in million dollars]	Budget Year - Eastern Region				
	Q1	Q2	Q3	Q4	Total
Beginning Backlog	10	11	17	19	10
Bookings	66	73	71	75	285
Revenues	65	67	69	71	272
End Backlog	11	17	19	23	23

[in million dollars]	Budget Year - International Sales				
	Q1	Q2	Q3	Q4	Total
Beginning Backlog	10	10	16	25	10
Bookings	62	70	74	75	281
Revenues	62	64	65	68	259
End Backlog	10	16	25	32	32

I point to my audience.

"I know that you must all be somewhat shocked. Those are high targets. Please refer to these numbers as first draft estimates only. We will all be working with you closely in the coming weeks to close it all, and to agree with you on the numbers. My goal is to give you a high target for orders. For those of you who have calculated this already, you will notice that the totals sum up to around ten percent higher than the company budget. This will be my buffer. And we will be talking a lot about buffers and buffer management today."

"Roger, what's the point in talking," says Eric from our Central Region. "It seems that you are pretty decisive on what you want. The numbers are pretty clear."

"Eric, I appreciate your honesty and straightforwardness." I knew there would be a cost associated with what I am trying to do. However, knowing the potential benefits, I am ready to pay the price. "All I am asking you is to be patient. I am aware that the previous budget process always included a bottom-up first. I do respect the bottom-up approach. The issue that I'm currently dealing with is that I want to propose a completely new way of managing the incentives next year. I prefer to invest all my efforts in this new way, rather than in the traditional lengthy bottom-up and then top-down approach that we had in the past years."

Gary jumps in, "Roger, can you proceed."

Could Gary be losing his patience? Usually, he is a strong believer in processes. Perhaps he is not convinced by my new approach.

"In all the years that I have dealt with targets and incentive plans," I proceed as requested, "there has always been an inherent conflict. On the one hand, whenever you receive a target, you want it to be as low as possible. The lower the target is, the higher the chances are that you will meet it, maybe even surpass it, and the higher the payoff. On the other hand, a high target is something to aspire to. It's what makes people advance up the organizational ladder. It makes our blood flow faster. It's like adrenaline. It also brings prestige and a strong feeling of contribution to the company's growth."

"Roger, let's face it," this is Eric again, "of course we always push the target as low as possible. With all due respect to prestige and the company, our payoff is our payoff. This is our job, it's what we do, and it's why we get up in the morning."

"Exactly, Eric. Nevertheless, we have done this the same way for many years. We have all assumed that this is an axiom, a truth accepted by everybody, and that this cannot, and certainly will not, be changed. Well, ladies and gentlemen, I am hereby challenging that. I think the existing approach is causing us undue damage, and thus I wish to change it once and for all."

"And how exactly you plan to do that?" This is John, from the Northwest. I am happy that he is alert and not too jet-lagged after a redeye flight from San Jose, California.

"Just a moment, I am not finished, John. Not yet. There is one more thing that I want to deal with. Has anybody here heard about the end-of-quarter syndrome?" They all laugh. They all relate to the end-of-quarter syndrome as nature's phenomenon. I'm not giving up yet. I now have their full attention.

"After that teaser, I am sorry to make a break here. I need to establish some foundation. Barry Kahn, our company consultant is here with us. After our break, Barry will make a short presentation about buffer management in projects.

Yes, I know you are in Sales, not in Engineering, but I need to give you some background information. We will then move to the analogy in Sales. I know this all sounds a bit theoretical, but we really need some foundation to overcome those so-called truths that we've been living with for ages now." They all stand up and grab a coffee or soda. I notice a lot of skepticism in their eyes. That's okay with me. I like these challenges. Managing change is perhaps what I like the most about my job.

* * *

Chapter 8
New Sales Incentives

November 16, Year 2

Nobody's better than Barry; the guy knows how to present an issue: "For many years now, projects in all domains—R&D, new products developments, construction, and all kinds of implementation projects have missed on all three of the main parameters of any project: budget, time and specifications. When projects run overtime, they typically run over budget, too, and we are forced to compromise on the specs."

"TOC has attempted to look at that never-ending problem and put an end to it. Books have been written on the methodology, and courses are now offered throughout the world on this new project management methodology, called Critical Chain Project Management or CCPM, for short. Sophisticated software tools now exist to help Engineering departments implementing CCPM in their projects. We use it at CGS, and I must say, with considerable success. In the next few minutes I will attempt to explain the main principles of the methodology."

Barry is now presenting TOC in project management to my team. He's clearly in his element. This is a good foundation for what's coming next – a new incentive plan scheme for the sales organization at CGS.

Barry continues, "the former project management methodology was based on putting all the tasks of a project on some type of chart. It included a careful estimate for the duration of each task. The longest chain of tasks, in terms of time, was usually considered as the time needed to complete the entire project. Moreover, this particular chain – the longest sequence of tasks, according to the logical flow of events, was the focus of managerial attention because of its critical impact on the duration of all projects. It was called the Critical Path, and it enjoyed clear priority in the assignment of the resources.

"A structured methodology, based upon these ideas, was called CPM, which stands for Critical Path Method, and it became the standard staple of project management all over the world. This all made sense, but still, almost none of the projects made it on time. After a careful analysis of the core problems of the past methodology, TOC basically offered two changes: the time to complete a project is not based solely on the longest chain of sequential tasks according to the logic of the project, but on the longest chain of tasks, which takes also into account organization's scarcity of resources; this is the *Critical Chain*." Seeing their puzzled expression, Barry explains: "See, logical sequence means that I first have to drill a hole and only after it's done can I start transferring a wire through the bore. That's the logic of the sequence. I can't do the second activity before the first one was accomplished. No way. However, sometimes I have to drill two holes. If I had two drills, I would do it in parallel. However, if all I have is one drill – I'll do it sequentially, even if there is no logical connection between the two holes. It's the logistics – shortage of drills – not the logic, which dictates that these two jobs have to be performed sequentially. Indeed, as so often happens in many projects, the same resource has to deal with more than one single task. Moreover, some resources are involved in more than one single project. Eventually, some resources become scarce, and the project duration will be adversely impacted by their limited availability. And we all realize that some activities can be done in parallel from a logical point of view, but due to scarcity of resources are done sequentially, and this often leads to project duration increases.

"The chain of activities made by those resources does not necessarily consist of a sequence of logically followed steps! Once fully understood, the Critical Chain can be much better managed. The four steps of constraint management apply here fully: Identify the Critical Chain, Exploit it, Subordinate all other tasks to it, and - as much as possible - Elevate it.

"Now comes the second important change: the past way to add safety to the process was to increase the estimated length of the tasks that were considered more risky. In fact, engineers were always very proud of themselves if they could negotiate as much safety as possible for their task. This would significantly decrease the chances of failing to be on time. Remember, sometimes, when the whole project is late and the budget starts to run short, management looks at the causes of delay with a very close eye and you don't want to be in the hot spot!

"The new method suggests a completely different way of managing projects' safety. The reasoning is as follows: for whatever reasons, all safety is almost always utilized fully. It is very rare that someone has safety and will not use it by either bringing his own task to near perfection, or in many cases, by starting slowly or even late – knowing that there is plenty of time. Not because he or she is lazy, not at all. There is always work waiting to be done, and safety times provide opportunity to do it. So the safety is always used, quite often upfront.

"But then, hey, there are the surprises—they always come and they are always bad! Those are the tasks that run over the assigned time because of unexpected problems. Now, if most of the tasks eat up all the safety time, and then there are also a few bad surprises, the outcome is known to all: the project will definitely run late.

"The new way suggests three types of buffers. However, in order to create them, we have to remove the existing safety from each and every single task. It's done cooperatively with the people planning and executing the task, not as top-down command. Of course, this is easier said than done, but nevertheless it's achievable. Then the safety is aggregated in three types of buffers.

A. The Project Buffer. This is a buffer that is put at the very end of the Critical Chain. In a way, this is an aggregate of the small safety times that were once put in all the tasks of the Critical Chain. Obviously, this safety is now removed from the steps themselves.

B. The Feeding Buffer. There are many paths of tasks that lead into the Critical Chain. When a non-critical chain is delayed, and does not enable progress in the Critical Chain, this non-critical chain can become critical unnecessarily. A feeding buffer is put just before the entry of a non-critical chain to a Critical Chain. This feeding buffer can be considered as a kind of project buffer of that specific non-critical chain. Here too, the buffer is an aggregate, composed mainly from the safety of each of the tasks of the non-critical chain.

C. The Resource Buffer. This is a different type of buffer. You can consider this as a mobilization order - *be ready when needed* - an advance notice for critical resources. When the resource buffer button is hit, the critical resources need to prepare themselves because the 'potato' that is coming to them is very hot; they can't simply let it wait and become cold. They need to be ready to do whatever needs to be done the moment it arrives.

"This is the TOC project management philosophy in a nutshell. It all becomes much more complicated in a multi-project environment, but that's not important now. Any questions?"

"I have one," says Nancy, the HR person. "How do the people in charge of the steps or tasks give up on their safety, and what happens to them when they are late?"

"Well, that's two questions. The first one, Nancy, is the million-dollar question. Our experience shows that once an organization accepts the new methodology, and once they incorporate the tools that come with it, what you mention becomes the most difficult challenge. Because they all share a common buffer and it is perfectly okay to be late, this may cause people to consume the common buffer in a frivolous way. However, the bottom line, Nancy, is that over time and after all people are educated, or, you may say re-educated, people understand that they are expected to provide aggressive, but achievable 'safetyless' times.

"Relating to your second question, there is no punishment whatsoever for being late. Let's all remember what we had in the past: all tasks were exhausting their safety, and a few steps were using more than their safety, resulting in late projects, by definition. Now we have the following paradigm: many tasks are on time; and a few tasks are running late; some of them are even very late, thus consuming the large common buffers, without exhausting them totally. If that's what happens, this results in the whole project being on time.

"The reason why so many tasks are on time, even without a safety added, is more of your domain, Nancy. I mean that this is part of human psychology." I can see that Nancy likes this approach. No wonder, she comes from this particular field. "When you know that you don't have enough time, you will start early, and you will work hard from the very beginning. More than that, you will be less prone to what I call as 'unnecessary creativity,' and you will make more sound compromises. This is what we need in project management.

"We all know that the result of a whole project can be near perfect, even if not every element is perfect in the same way. You see, a car can be perfect even if one of the electric cables inside it is two inches longer than it could have been given more time to work on the car's electrical cabling design. A software program can be quite good and relatively bug-free, even if it has ten thousand lines of code, instead of eight thousand lines of code which it could have if given more time to optimize some of its routines. Is this clear now?" They all kind of nod. This is not easy stuff to swallow in less than an hour. But I have to strike while the iron is hot. I take over for Barry now.

"So, what is the analogy? How does this all affect our sales organization?"

"The only direct analogy I can see," says Eric "is what you mentioned in your introduction, Roger. The engineers used to negotiate the time of their tasks, very much like my sales force negotiates their annual or quarterly quota – fiercely. Similarly, those who negotiated a better quota for themselves had a tendency to not work as hard in the beginning of the quarter. They had a tendency to be in a relaxed and overconfident mode."

"Another analogy," says Pierce, "is in the surprises. More than once, I have seen our best sales person in our most lucrative territory fail because of something completely unexpected. The last one was the sudden bankruptcy of that company DTL. They were about to order multiple pieces of equipment. Their CEO was overconfident, and suddenly – nothing. Nada. Zero!"

"My analogy," adds Gary, "is in the compromises. Projects, perhaps, compromise on specs. In sales, we compromise on terms and conditions. We all know that at the year-end we give higher discounts, grant better payment terms, agree to longer warranty periods, and so on, and so forth. If we were on target with our sales, or we thought we'd be on target, we would compromise much less."

"Bingo, Gary!" This one was unexpected, but it's a good one. It's not for nothing this guy is our CEO. And you can tell his background is in Sales. "Now that some of the analogies are clear, I want to propose a new set of goals for all. For the Eastern Region, for example, it would look as follows:

[in M$'s]	Budget Year - Eastern Region													
	1	2	3	4	5	6	7	8	9	10	11	12	Annual Buffer	Total
Bookings	30	30	30	30	30	30	30	30	30	30	30	30	75	285

As you saw, I moved to a month-by-month system, rather than a quarter-by-quarter. I need a better resolution than the existing quarterly one. Eric, can you generate orders of thirty million dollars or more every month?"

"Roger, in the BBS you showed before, our highest quarterly bookings were seventy five million per quarter, and this was in Q4. Until today, our highest quarterly number has been seventy million dollars. That's less than twenty four million a month. And you want thirty per month from the very beginning. The answer is simply, no!"

"Okay, Eric, okay. I understand what you're saying. But can you and your staff fight for it? By the way, none of your personal incentive plans will be based on the thirty million per month. I am telling you that up-front; it's okay not to achieve it. We simply want to work together on seeing how we can eventually achieve it. We definitely want to achieve it. But again, we are okay if you don't."

"Roger, I am a bit confused. You want me to sell thirty million a month, but it's okay if I don't? What happens if I'm unable to reach this thirty million mark? What is the incentive package based on?"

"For you, as a manager, there will be some qualitative measures, but in terms of numbers, there will be only one: the annual target of two hundred and eighty five million dollars. You and I will constantly look at the buffer. Its size at the beginning of the year is seventy five million; the difference between three hundred and sixty million (12x30) and the annual goal of two hundred and eighty five million. As long as the buffer remains above fifty million dollars, you will not even hear from me — you are on your own."

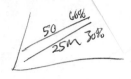

"However, when the buffer is below fifty million, please book your flight and come and see me, as we have some serious talking to do. With a buffer below twenty five million dollars, I am expecting urgent actions from you! However, if in one of the months, you achieve twenty million instead of thirty million that is okay. I do understand that. As you know, bookings start from zero every month. So there is no longer any time to rest. You and your staff will need to start working like crazy from the first available minute in the month. Every month. You and your staff will not rest even if you exceed the monthly goal. After all, there is a buffer to protect."

"And what about CGS?" asks Gary.

"Our monthly booking goal is set at one hundred and ten million dollars, with an annual buffer of two hundred and thirty five million."

"Roger, you must be kidding." Eliza is with us now. "CGS has never had a month of bookings that comes even close to the one hundred million dollars. One hundred and ten is unachievable, period."

Well, if this is even hard for Eliza to grasp, it must either be a very innovative idea, or my explanations stink. Or both. Probably both. So I try to be positive:

"That's perfectly okay, Eliza. This means that we will be eating our buffer every single month. Nevertheless, my staff and I will work as hard as we possibly can to protect our buffer month by month. As long as our buffer remains above one hundred and sixty, we will run the business smoothly. Below one hundred and sixty, we will all regroup, as our target is in danger of not being met. Below eighty, we need to take drastic emergency measures."

"Roger, I am worried about attrition." This is John from Central. "We will be working at a pace never seen before in Sales. You are right, the third month of the quarter is when we work the hardest, but at least in the first month of the quarter we can recuperate and put our thoughts together. Believe me, after every quarter end, I really need a few days, and my staff does, too. With an unachievable monthly booking target, for every single month of the year, we may not be able to hold the pace."

"I agree with John." Nancy is now speaking from her HR position. "This will kill our organization."

"Don't exaggerate, Nancy," I try to pacify her. However, I'm not very successful.

"I'm not exaggerating. A constant high speed pace can be detrimental to our people."

"Whenever we reach such a debate, and I have been in many of them in my career," Gary comes in to rescue me, "we assume that there is no management in the company. However, there is one, and there is a damned good one. If we face attrition, we'll manage it – period. I like the concept of pushing the organization to its limits while being alert to its ability to cope with those limits. More often than not, the people rise to the challenge and there is no need to reduce it artificially.

"You know what they say: 'Shoot for the moon – even if you miss, you are still among stars.' However, if we see that the situation starts to get dangerous, we can always lower the bar. My guess is that this will not be needed. People like to be challenged, especially sales people."

"But what about the customers, Gary? Sometimes, people tend to forget that in order to create bookings, some customer needs to submit a purchase order somewhere!" Pierce represents the voice of the customer. "We can develop all these nice theories, but we need customers to cooperate with this crazy thing."

"Pierce, what's the difference?" Gary is fast to respond and I sit quiet, enjoying every minute of it. I'm afraid I'm enjoying it too much. I hope it doesn't show. In a short while Pierce is going to be my boss; I'd better not show how I think about his grasp of the situation. Gary continues: "What's so different? Aren't we still fighting like hell to get those purchase orders? We are, aren't we?

"The only thing that we ask now is that the effort is done on a constant basis. I do remember what Barry said about the human factor: 'when you know that you don't have enough time, you will start early and you will work hard from the very beginning. More than that, you will become less unnecessarily creative, and will make many more sound compromises and decisions. This is exactly what we need in sales today. The new method gives this a good chance."

"Roger, I still want to ask one simple question," Eliza diverts the discussion to another direction. "This is your thought process: you learned a lot from the implementation of TOC in project management, you found proper analogies in the sales process, and you want to implement some type of buffer management in sales, accordingly."

"Yes, Eliza, that is more or less correct. So what is your question?"

"I am getting to it, Roger. In TOC for project management, Barry referred to two elements: the Critical Chain, and buffer management. Critical Chain being the focal point of managerial attention, while buffer management was the control mechanism. I can see that while you have implemented buffer management somehow, you have not touched upon the Critical Chain at all. Why is this? Don't you need to define something similar to it in sales?"

"That's an excellent question, Eliza, really. In many ways, we have done it already. For example, not too long ago, we discovered that our sales-support staff was becoming a critical resource, and they slowed down the whole process of generating sales. They were doing what we call bad multi-tasking. We have focused our improvement effort there, and I believe that we have solved that at this point." I hope I sound convincing on this matter, as I haven't spoken to Chuck in Toronto in quite a while. But, knowing him, if there were still problems with the sales support staff, I'd know it by now. I continue: "Beforehand, as you may recall, we had focused on the Production Demo stage. Eliza, we are learning every day. I am sure there will be more to it as we proceed. But we clearly see a chain of activities which, at the end, produces the cash created by sales."

We proceed with the meeting, and we try to close on some more details of the new approach. I think that my staff bought in. I am grateful to Gary for having helped me in the critical moments. What will happen next year, when Pierce is the CEO? Better not think about it now.

*   *   *

Lizzie and I are on the move this weekend to buy a new computer for our home. The one we have now is more than four years old, and it doesn't run some of the new games or new applications that Lizzie or Jennifer want to use. First, we spend a few hours on the net. We look at the prices and the configurations.

Very quickly, Lizzie takes control over the mouse. I am not clicking fast enough for her. I am amazed by how natural this all is for her. I remember that I learned the basic operations of Windows when I was over twenty. Lizzie has grown up with it since she was two years old. It has all become part of her. She doesn't even need to think about it, it all comes naturally and damned fast, too. We argue about the need for a more expensive flat panel display. She looks at me as if I am coming from another planet.

"Dad, we can't have one of those huge monitors in our house anymore. They're noisy, they take up the better part of the desk, and the quality is not good enough."

"Not good enough for what?"

"Dad, you know that I plan to edit our videos on the computer. I need to have a good resolution. I also need to have the right video boards." I look at my daughter and I feel like I'm from the Middle Ages. In history, not in my age. I'd better not argue.

"Okay, a flat panel it is. Seventeen inches is enough, I guess."

"Dad, please, minimum is nineteen inches, and twenty-one is preferred."

"Why?" I ask, not even thinking about the hit my credit card will take this weekend with this new purchase.

"Well, because the computers nowadays have a DVD player and we all may want to watch movies on the computer whenever our TV set and DVD player is taken by another member of the family."

"Nineteen inches it is," I say, hoping that we are done.

After some more searching online, Lizzie decides that we should shop for them in person before making a final decision. So we go to one of the computer chains and look at the different models. Lizzie is the one who is doing all the talking. She talks the 'megabyte' language as if it were her mother tongue. I just watch.

She decides to pick some accessories too: a camera - for video conferencing – she says; a high quality color printer – for printing our digital images; a color scanner – absolutely mandatory, according to my lovely daughter. What can I say; I make my living out of selling scanners, so how can I refuse. Needless to say that we also walk through the software department, where Lizzie picks the newest video editing software package, and one or two of the newest PC games.

When we leave, we somehow end up with a $3,000 plus bill. And all I wanted was to buy a one-thousand-dollar computer. I guess those are the wonders of consumer behavior. Sometimes,

I am happy that I am in the business of marketing and selling capital equipment to the manufacturing environment. At least, in business we always know that there will be reasons for a buy. Then I think again, is it really different from Lizzie's reasons? Let's see? Usually it's one or more out of the three reasons for a buy: (a) capacity – a new, additional manufacturing line is required and more capacity is needed; or simply existing capacity isn't sufficient – there is a bottleneck and buying our equipment can elevate it; (b) technology – the current manufacturer's equipment is unable to produce at the new levels of technology, and new, more modern equipment is required; and finally (c) replacement or displacement. Replacement is mostly for old equipment that is no longer reliable enough, or that has become obsolete because of age. Displacement takes place when a new technology, disruptive to the existing one is offered, a technology that shifts the paradigm of a current process. In our industry, 'computer to printing plate' displaced the previous 'computer to film to printing plate' process to a large extent.

My experience shows that the easiest sale is the capacity sale. With bottleneck capacity, a good ROI study usually makes the deal. Technology is usually more difficult. Replacement is the most difficult, but not completely impossible. With displacement, it depends on many aspects. It can either be a very easy sale, or an extremely difficult one. All those thoughts go through my mind as I start to load the huge boxes in the trunk of my car. I can hardly close it. I can't believe how much stuff we got for the money we paid, after all. I prefer not to think about Joanna's face. We went out to buy a PC, and we're back with a video production studio. Perhaps I'll let Lizzie do the talking again, she is so good at it.

*   *   *

Just after the meeting on the new incentive scheme, Eliza came to see me and said that she wanted to talk to me about the whole issue. Although I updated the management team well ahead of time, and I know that Eliza was certainly not surprised in that meeting, this is not a good sign. Eliza is what I call a strong CFO. CFOs are always caught up in the middle: are they protecting the business, or are they supporting it? When sales started to go down, more than a year ago, Pierce put a lot of pressure on Eliza to recognize revenues with less tight restraints. She didn't budge one inch. Also, Eliza is very harsh on provisions. Whenever she feels that a customer is not creditworthy, she does not hesitate to increase the provisions made for future bad debt.

When sales are going up, nobody really cares. However, when sales are going down, the pressure on the CFO is huge. We all knew what a decrease in sales would mean to the share price, and from that to the personal wealth of all of us. Eliza did not care, even though she is a shareholder as much as every other member of management, perhaps even more. At that time, she wore only one hat on her head—the one that protects the business. She has all my respect for that. At the same time, when I came to her with the new incentive scheme, she wore the 'supporting-the-business' hat. She really tries to help and to facilitate changes.

Anyway, a few days later, as I sit in her office, I remind her that she wanted to talk about the new incentive scheme.

"Yes, Roger, thanks for coming by. While I listened to your presentation to sales management, a fear, or rather, a concern, came up."

"I am all ears, Eliza." I don't like this. I surely don't. I hope that it will be possible to overcome her concerns. I have already gone quite far in this process. I feel that there is a buy-in of our sales people. There is no way back, not for me.

"You see, Roger, when the sales people are under huge pressure to bring in orders, there is, over time, a tendency to bring in less-healthy orders. By less healthy I mean orders that may, for example, not be turned into cash over time, for a multitude of reasons."

"Eliza, you know that we will take drastic measures against whoever acts unethically at CGS."

"I know, Roger. I've seen sales people who asked their customers-friends to place an order one quarter and have those orders cancelled just prior to shipment a few months later. They did it in order to help the sales person meet his, or her, booking target in a difficult quarter. But I am not talking about that now. I don't think that we have such problems at CGS any longer. Thank God. I am talking about what Pierce often used to call 'creative sales.'"

"Such as?"

"Well, Roger, you've been in Sales long enough to have seen it all. There are so many examples. The most common one is delayed payments, sometimes by over a year. Another one is the addition of acceptance criteria that are often difficult to meet, and subsequently lead to further post-sale discounts needed to secure some compromised acceptance and future payments. Another one in a guarantee of discounts for future purchases, a kind of rebate coupon.

"A last example is the promise of an upgrade or future feature in a new software version. We have all seen that happen too many times. The issue is that the higher the pressure, the more of those cases we see, and the less healthy our bookings stream becomes. Every single order becomes an exception."

"I see what you mean, but I think that this is remedied by our incentive plans."

"How is that?"

"Well, there are two fundamental reasons why sales people work hard. The first one is prestige or pride. Sales guys, at the least the good ones, love to compete. It is in their blood. When they get a target, they want to reach it, and be winners. They want to be better than their peers.

"The second one is the monetary payoff. Sales guys consider themselves as business people, for just cause. If they have an opportunity to make more money, they will not let it go! All what I presented to my sales management had to do with the first part – the pride or prestige or competition part – whatever you prefer to call it. The second part, the monetary one, is completely different. Our sales people will get commission on cash."

"Which means?"

"Their commission is paid to them only when customers pay us. Their commission is not received on bookings, it is not received on revenues, it is not received on completion of installation, and it is not even received on customers' acceptance of our machines. It is received only when we are paid, i.e., on cash received!"

"Roger, you mean that delayed payment, or any type of conditional element, whether acceptance-related or engineering-related, affects them as much as it affects the company?"

"I don't know if 'as much as us,' but they are certainly affected."

"This may mean that there may sometimes be a very long lag between the time they take an order and the time they see the money."

"Yes, that is correct. By the way, it's the same for CGS. Of course, we may sometimes make advance payments toward future commissions, for those who are in need. But the principle remains as is: they are due their commission in full 'on cash received.'"

"Roger, go ahead with your plan. I am behind it one hundred percent."

"Thanks, Eliza, your support is critical to me."

*   *   *

Chapter 9
The Cash Machine

December 10, Year 2

"Barry, I have put a lot of thought into what you have done for us in the last year or so. Along the way, I have drawn my own conclusions. I would like to share that with you. By the way, is this a good time for you?" I am wondering how this TOC expert will react to my own TOC thought process. I suddenly feel like I'm a student again!

"Sure, go ahead. Give it to me."
"Well, I see four main processes in an organization like ours:
(1) Production;
(2) R&D or Engineering;
(3) the process that actually generates the cash – I don't know yet how to call this one; and
(4) Customer Service." Barry's face remains indifferent. I wonder if I'm making some inroads here or not?

"That's an interesting way to put it," he says. No doubt, he must come from the field of psychotherapy.

"While most TOC applications are implemented in production, project management or engineering, TOC is less often implemented in the cash generating process and, I would say, almost never in customer support or post-sale services. At least, that's my impression."

"Well, that doesn't mean it isn't done. You see, some call TOC 'The best kept secret of the management field,'" he smiles. Then he continues: "Roger, let's call this 'cash generating process' of yours a 'Cash Machine.' Okay?"

"Thanks, Barry," it seems that I have his attention now. And I definitely like the term Cash Machine. "The main reason for not hearing often about the Cash Machine is because it is spread across multiple functions or disciplines. It is never presented, at least at the companies I know, as an integrated mechanism such as other processes are. Everybody understands that the various elements of Production are just parts of the whole. In the Cash Machine, however, they are spread all over among different functions and responsibilities. In a way, I could picture the various elements of the Cash Machine as follows:"

Function	Process
Marketing	Awareness creation
	Interest incitement
	Knowledge transfer
	Lead generation
Sales	Qualification
	Needs assessment
	Letter of Understanding
	Presentation demo
	Solution proposal/technical check
	Production demo
	Quotation submission
	Negotiation
	Closing
Order Administration	Order received/basic checks

	Approval cycle
	Equipment allocation
	Product integration/customization per customer order, testing and packing
	Submission of installation call for customer services
	Shipping
Finance	Invoicing
Customer Support	Unpacking
	Installation of separate stations
	Networking of all stations
	Application and workflow set-up
	Customer training
	Acceptance test
Finance	Cash Collection

I continue:

"Surprisingly, if we look at it as a single, continuous process, this is exactly like a production chain: a sequence of steps, with a high level of interdependence among the steps, and with a certain level of uncertainty that each step will be achieved on time. There is raw material (prospects), work in progress (customer orders), and there are the finished goods (cash). There are many buffers in front resources and..." Now I wait to see if I created some suspense in this block of ice.

"I am still all ears," Barry seems definitely interested.

"...and there are bottlenecks that should be exploited, then elevated and so on. When you look at all departments separately, you don't have a view over the whole Cash Machine. Of course, it interacts with the other three processes – Engineering, Production and Customer Support. And this interaction can be sometimes very interactive indeed. But still, it is a separate process, interacting with the others in the same way we interact with our suppliers or distributors. We depend on them, they depend on us, and yet – we are we and they are they: separate entities interacting for common good.

The same is correct for the Cash Machine within the confines of the same organization. What we were, knowingly or intuitively, able to achieve in the course of the last two years is the implementation of a complete TOC process over the Cash Machine of Carmen Graphics Solutions."

"Roger, you mean that we managed a few iterations in the process. You remember that this is a never-ending process."

"I know that very well, Barry. The question that I'm raising is: when does the market become the constraint and not one of the internal steps."

"I see what you mean. As long we have an internal constraint, say a bottleneck in production, it is all up to you – managers in the company – to elevate that bottleneck and increase the 'cash producing capacity' of the company. When the constraint is in the market, it all becomes a market development challenge – which is also a manageable one, by the way – but of a different type. In the first case the constraint is an internal one, under our full control, and thus we can impact it much easier. When the constraint is an external one, say the market, our ability to impact it, while still existing, must take into account the behavior of our clients, our competitors, sometimes even events on the global scene. So Roger, what do you think, have you done this already? Have you increased the internal 'cash producing capacity' of CGS to a point where you have moved the constraint to the market?"

"Barry, what do you think? Have we? Is there a way to know?"

"I suggest we think about it." He is back to his shrink manner. Well, maybe it is better this way. At least it gives me the feeling that the ideas are mine, and not of some external guru. Barry continues, "Maybe I can raise the concept with Gary in my meeting tomorrow. After all, while you have an important role in the functioning of CGS's Cash Machine, it is Gary who is ultimately in charge of that machine."

"You're right. Thanks for listening to me. I appreciate it."

"My pleasure, Roger."

I wonder what Barry and Gary will talk about in their meeting. I kind of feel a bit awkward. I've been in the business for many years. I have my MBA and have taken some Executive Education programs at some of the most prestigious institutions in the world. Fortunately enough they are all in our backyard, here in the Boston area. Still, I have never heard about anything similar to the Cash Machine. Why don't others look at it that way? Do the five constraint steps work here as well? I mean identify, exploit, subordinate, elevate - and start all over again. Am I the first one to identify that process and to implement that methodology? I can't be. Have we overcome all internal bottlenecks at CGS? Or maybe we are working on expanding the capacity of non-constrained resources - and thereby wasting our time and money? There are so many questions that are going through my head but at the end – Barry is right, this is more of Gary's problem. After all, I am just in charge of Sales, am I not?

*   *   *

I remain bothered with my conclusions throughout the week. Then I remember our production chief, John, our VP of Operations. After all, he is the one who first implemented TOC in production several years ago. He should know about it more than anybody else. That is, at least in CGS. It was him who helped us to see the analogy between projects and sales. I give him the same spiel I gave to Barry. I am waiting for his response.

"Roger, what you're saying makes a lot of sense. It's funny, I never thought about it that way. It's perfectly clear to me that manufacturing is one single process, in spite of the fact it involves many functions in production, engineering, planning, material management, transportation and distribution. It also interacts with many external entities, like our suppliers and vendors, our clients and even our competitors. Of course, to apply this approach to your process you'll have to change a few terms. Like the 'ratio' in your 'funnel' is 'yield' in my world. Your 'time from prospect to close deal, or to cash' is like the 'lead time' in mine.

"John, I get it. My 'qualified prospects' are your 'raw materials,' and our 'cash' is like your 'sold finished goods.'"

"Exactly. There is not much conceptual difference."

"Let's see. Let me make a drawing on the board." I draw the standard funnel of sales.

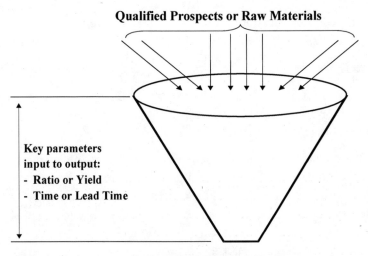

Qualified Prospects or Raw Materials

**Key parameters
input to output:
- Ratio or Yield
- Time or Lead Time**

Cash or Sold Finished Goods

"So, John, since you are so much more experienced in operational management and constraint thinking than I am, give me some tips." Since we already have made the analogy between the production world and the Cash Machine, let's push the envelope further; let's see what we can learn. John is visibly flattered that somebody from the white-collar world is ready to learn something from a blue-collar guy. His smile is hard to hide.

"Well, one big lesson is that reaching a local optimum in one area of the production floor does not really help to ship more finished goods, unless it's at a bottleneck. You see, many department or area managers make continuous improvements in their departments and areas, and they are very proud about it. The issue is that it doesn't help us one bit, unless they are in charge of the bottleneck resource. And it is very hard to convey that message to them."

"Right, John. I know exactly what you mean; I remember that when we increased the capacity of the Production Demos, we saw immediate results. But later on, we decided to increase the capacity of our ability to submit quotations to our customers. We invested a lot of efforts there. We even developed a sophisticated automatic quotation tool. This was quite time consuming, it was costly, and it worked beautifully. But then we discovered, I must admit, that it was all in vain. It didn't help to increase sales one bit. Now that I think about it, we're lucky that instead of dwelling on it, we immediately moved to the delivery process. I think that this was truly the next area to focus on. What else can we learn?"

"Another big lesson of TOC in Production is the formalization of the famous DBR mechanism: 'Drum, Buffer, Rope' or whatever you want to call it. It describes the way material moves on the production floor. This means that we release raw material to the floor only at the pace of the bottleneck. That's the Drum according to which beat the entire system marches. Buffer is a work-in-progress released into the system and awaiting processing in front of the bottleneck. It protects its smooth action even if resources feeding it are stuck for whatever reason. Rope is the mechanism that ties the introduction of additional material into the process to the pace of the work of the bottleneck. If it stops for whatever reason, we better stop the stream of the raw-materials; otherwise, we'll generate lots of work-in-progress that is not turned into sold or shipped finished goods."

"Yes, I know what you are talking about. We had the same problem with the Lilly. We got many customers, but we got stuck with too much work-in-progress. In other words, installations that we could not complete, and turn into cash. Who cares about that one? The marketing folks were happy as we got many orders. Unfortunately, the question 'so what?' applies here fully. What else, John, give me more." I am getting excited.

"Well, there are many, many lessons we learned from implementing TOC in production. Let me see. Another one is set-up. In order to improve local efficiencies, we worked with big batches; we used to produce a maximum amount of parts after a long set-up. Now, we do as many set-ups as needed in non-bottleneck resources, so that the bottleneck resource can be fully utilized."

"John, this is really intriguing. The analogy here may be that we can be more flexible with non-bottleneck resources. For example, we could have diverted our sales efforts from hardware sales to software sales. Indeed, in case our sales channels are no longer a bottleneck, we can spend some more time on missions that do not generate more 'work-in-progress' that gets stuck anyway. You see, if the bottleneck is our hardware installation capacity, we could divert non-bottleneck resources such as Sales to opportunities that do not necessitate hardware installation. Really, this all becomes so obvious now: there isn't much sense in pushing our guys to sell more machines, when we don't have resources to install them.

In any case installation capacity will limit our cash intake. But there isn't anything that prevents us from making more money from software sales."

"So why don't you do it?" John inquires.

"Well" I answer, "we usually don't do that because once we train our people to sell some hardware, we push them to do just that, in order to maximize their efficiency. At the same time, who cares if they aren't that efficient in selling hardware? This does not matter as long as we can't install the equipment and then generate cash from our sales. In a way, training to sell another type of product is equivalent to set-up time in production. That's another good one too. Give me one more, John, a good one please!"

"Well, I think that the best lesson of all is the fifth step in constraints management: start all over again. Don't let the inertia take control. This is a never-ending story."

"Yes, to a certain extent we did that, too. I think that we crossed all departments in the last twelve months. Frankly speaking, I think that we're entering into inertia mode now since I don't know what the next bottleneck is."

"This may well be, Roger. This happens often when a company approaches the first billion dollars in sales, as we are now. It is time for Gary and Ray to do something dramatic again. Usually, they've been able to pull a trick out of their hat at the right time. I wonder what it will be now."

"Yes, I am asking myself the question too. Thanks a lot, John. It was a pleasure as usual."

Now that we have a holistic grasp of the business, from the market, or prospects, all the way to cash, we can, theoretically at least, take more or most cash from our marketplace. If we become good at it, we could increase our yield as well. Yield is more than just market share. It should include as part of the total market even the things to which today we don't even relate, like the business lost because customers decide to postpone their business.

*   *   *

At CGS, Eliza our CFO, is also responsible for our IT infrastructure. Most companies have long since appointed a Chief Information Officer, or CIO, at the company management level. But CGS is rather lean in our managerial structure, especially at the C level (all the Chief *Something* Officers). At CGS, Gary has preferred to keep IT under Eliza. She is simply good at it. She has a good technological grasp and even more, she has that ability to (a) implement difficult projects, and (b) identify enterprise solutions that are not mature enough or ready to be implemented.

She is the one who recommended to progress very slowly with full-scale CRM solutions. We have all the bits and bytes, like our sales tracking system, but all the applications that deal with customers are not fully integrated yet. I decide to spend some time with Eliza, asking her to wear her IT hat for this meeting. I present the whole Cash Machine approach to her. I am obviously quite excited. When I put the whole sequential process on the board, I add a column on the right: $ Value in millions of dollars.

Function	Process	$ Value
Marketing	Awareness creation	1,000
	Interest incitement	800
	Knowledge transfer	800
	Lead generation	600
Sales	Qualification	470

	Needs assessment	450
	Letter of Understanding	450
	Presentation demo	400
	Solution proposal/technical check	360
	Production demo	300
	Quotation submission	280
	Negotiation	200
	Closing	100
Order Administration	Order received/basic checks	100
	Approval cycle	100
	Equipment allocation	120
	Product integration/ customization per customer order, testing and packing	120
	Submission of installation call for customer services	
	Shipping	120
Finance	Invoicing	105
Customer Support	Unpacking	70
	Installation of separate stations	50
	Networking of all stations	50
	Application and workflow set-up	50

	Customer training	40
	Acceptance test	40
Finance	Cash Collection	30

"Eliza, this is just an example of a possible status snapshot at a certain time, let's say at the end of the second month of a year. Listen, I'm not sure if I should be the one discussing this. I think that only the CEO should do this, as he is in charge of, among others, marketing, sales, finance, operations and customer support. But look at the status snapshot anyway. This is a reflection of what the Cash Machine is working on from the beginning of a year until the end of the second month. It shows the scope of business which each of its components was facing, or dealing with, during that period. It does not relate to orders taken prior to that, as this would appear in a different report. I guess that this report might be typical of a time prior to us solving the implementation projects' length issue. Look at the picture above. It is a simple status snapshot, but it says so much about the whole organization."

"Yes, Roger, it does say a lot. The first thing that jumps out is that the installation phase does not support the cash-generation that most, or all, other components of our Cash Machine are currently able to support. But you just said that. What's even more important from the corporate point of view is the dramatic drop from the potential market we see to the actual beginning of the sales cycle in the ten steps-of-sale. It drops by more than half. And then, within our sales steps, we lose another three quarters of the potential. Perhaps this is natural, but it is nevertheless worth the while investigating."

"Eliza, I think that we could talk for hours about that. During my entire career, the handover between the different functions in a company has always been so unclear. And even when it was clear, the capacity balancing between the different functions was almost never done, at least not adequately and proactively. Do you think we could build that in into our IT system?"

"Roger, I will repeat what I have said thousands of times. The first step is never to build something into an IT system. The first step is to turn such a concept into an integral part of the company processes. Yes, I do believe that we can build the IT system around it, and yes, we can offer the online visibility that you are looking for. Still, we as a company need to adopt that approach in a comprehensive and integrated manner first. Have you talked about all of that with Gary? He is the one who defines CGS' business processes. You have just said that it's a CEO's job. So we'll have to turn to Gary first. I'm sure he will like it. After all, you have gained a lot of credibility with all your new ideas in the last year or so."

"Thanks, but I have left that to Barry Kahn. He said he would present the Cash Machine concept to Gary. This was a few weeks ago. I haven't heard back from him and haven't had time to ask him about it yet. You know that I am very busy with closing the year and preparing for next year. Our targets are super aggressive, as you know."

"I am certain that Gary cannot remain indifferent to the Cash Machine approach. You'll hear from him for sure."

"I am sure about this one, too. Thanks for listening to me."

"My pleasure, Roger."

*   *   *

Chapter 10
Even Hotter

February 5, Year 3

We had a great sales kick-off meeting. It is always good to bring all the sales people together. This was my second kick-off as VP of Sales. This year we invited our reps too. They are, after all, an integral part of our sales force by now. The atmosphere was great. Gary made a great inaugural speech. Believe me, he knows how to do it. I wonder, who in CGS will be able to deliver such a speech when he is gone? We gave awards to our best performing sales people, and we also gave some awards to what I call 'special cases' – most innovative deal-getter; the rookie of the year; the one who sold most Lilly scanners – this is after the re-launch, of course.

At some time, during the last evening, we asked all non-quota bearing employees to leave, and I introduced the new sales incentives scheme. I did my best to explain it gradually. To leave a sweet taste in their mouths, I also announced a ten-percent increase in the variable portion of each and every sales person's package. In other words, if they make their annual target, they'll get more money than what they got this year. This gives a big boost to the over-achievers too.

Unlike when I presented the incentive plans to my guys, now – this is a non-negotiable thing. You, as a sales person, can either take it, and make the best out of it, or else you opt out of the game, one way or another. The funniest part is that later, at the summary session, some complained that the kick-off meeting had taken too much of their time. To make their monthly booking goal, they each need to close at least one deal. From mid-January till the end of it does not leave a lot of time! Also, I would guess that many customers used up their budget by the end of December. But this is exactly what I want: an early start, no time to rest, zero complacency.

*　　*　　*

Joanna, Lizzie, Jennifer and I spend the weekend on the slopes, skiing like crazy, till exhaustion. Joanna used some of the option money to buy me a new set of skis and boots. I was lucky. From the day Joanna and I had our discussion on whether to exercise or not, until the exercise day in that same week, on Thursday, the share price jumped from $40 to$45. Yes indeed, for 15,000 options this is a nice addition of $75,000. The new skis are a fair bonus. Ray, Gary and the Board have not decided yet how to allocate the options to management for this year yet. They'll have to do so very soon. I hope that we will be spoiled this year.

*　　*　　*

I am back in Southern California, with Joe, the District Sales Manager, and his team. I have come to meet with an important prospect for Q1, or perhaps I should say for February bookings. Joe suggested that I come and sit with them at the weekly sales meeting in which they review all accounts among all team members. After all, this is where the whole new incentive scheme started with the infamous brainstorming session. It may be a nice opportunity to close the loop and I immediately accepted Joe's invitation. After the usual introduction, Joe starts reviewing all Sales Executives' achievements.

"Well, let's start. Ladies first Laura, you have failed in meeting your quota in January, and February does not look too good. In January, you were only at eighty percent of your quota, and in February, unless a miracle happens, you won't get to one hundred percent either. Luckily we have Roger here, and perhaps you can explain to all of us, and to him as well, what you plan to do about it."

Wow, I can't believe my ears. Joe, as talented as he is as a sales manager, didn't get it at all! Under normal circumstances I would usually never do this, but now I have no choice; the stakes are simply too high, I need to interfere.

"Joe, allow me stop you right here. I am really sorry. I simply think that there is a misunderstanding and I am glad that I have the opportunity to clarify things in front of everybody. In fact I may have to thank you, because it is early enough to correct that misunderstanding throughout the whole company, if needed."

"Roger, what are you talking about?"

"Joe and everybody here – listen to me very carefully – there is a new paradigm, one which accepts that being under the monthly quota is okay. Yes, you hear me right; it's okay to be under the quota. Not that it is what we want to happen, but nonetheless, it's acceptable. It is built that way inherently. As you all realize, we've put a quota which is rather high, and that's an understatement. Your chances of achieving one hundred percent of it are – say - with a probability of fifty to sixty percent. This also means that the chances of missing the quota are with a probability of forty to fifty percent. That is very high, but again, that is okay." The room is now very silent. They listen carefully.

Joe looks doubtful: "So how should we as managers react to not meeting a quota? In the past we used to consider a performance lay off for repeatedly missing a quota. This is not Engineering, where they can always be late and nothing happens to them.

This is Sales, and here we like to compete and achieve our targets – always!"

"Joe, I count on you and everybody else to do everything, to use all your creativity and talents, to meet and to beat the quota month after month. I want to see a fighting spirit. I want to see a bleeding competition. Your quota is your goal – take it, beat it, exceed it. The success of the whole company is on your shoulders. Look left and right, without everybody fighting in the same way, our company cannot succeed. You are part of it.

"Yet, at the same time, managerially, we should treat anybody who does not meet the monthly quota in an almost forgiving way, and surely in a very supportive way. This isn't the case for somebody who eats up all his or her annual buffer and misses the whole year.

"Let me summarize how I see this: push and support your people to meet the quota. However, manage them through their buffer. Let them run without your interference until a third of the buffer is eaten up, be actively involved and support them beyond that. Take drastic measures when two thirds of the buffer is consumed, especially when this happens early in the year. At the same time, do not punish anyone for missing a monthly quota. Is that clear?"

"I think it is. By the way, what do you mean by 'drastic measures?'"

"Well, Joe, I don't have to teach this to you – do what all sales managers do: from reviewing terms and conditions of potential deals, to special promotions, through territory re-assignment. Sometimes, we assign a dedicated sales support person to a territory. Sometimes, we add a reseller. Sometimes, you can also ask the Regional Sales Manager or even me as VP of Sales to spend more time with a certain Sales Executive. I know that I have even asked Gary to help, and he gladly spends a week or two in a territory."

"Thanks, Roger. You see, I know I had to bring you to this meeting."

"By all means, Joe. Thanks for inviting me."

Joe starts the whole review again. He does it perfectly now. When I get out of the meeting, I immediately place a call to all Regional Sales Managers and then to all District Sales Managers. Luckily, all except for one more, got the concept beforehand. I spend at least an hour on the phone with the one who made the same mistake as Joe, and I think that I succeeded in delivering the message. Just in case, I schedule a visit in his region.

*   *   *

It's the last day of March already. We are running three months, a full quarter, with the new incentive scheme now. All I can say is that it's great. Everybody works like crazy all the time. Chris, my analyst, was able to program our sales tracking system so that I see the bookings per person, per district and per region, on a monthly basis. Also, I have a view of all the buffers in a similar way. In a nutshell, I can see who is consuming his buffer dangerously, and who is not. Q1 is still early enough in the year to take action. I have asked all sales management to spend two days at headquarters with me in March. They asked that at least one day of it take place during the weekend. After all, they have their eyes on the month of April already, and in a very cruel way, the meter for bookings resets to zero the first of every single month. But Gary was right. In spite of the pressure, there is virtually no attrition. At least none we can see. They see this as a challenge. They all know that we are leaving competition far behind. When the other guys are resting after a tough quarter, we are running at full speed. What is nice, too, is that as long as the Cash Machine works at a constant, nearly homogeneous, full speed mode all the time, the constraints are more visible than ever before. In the past the irregularities on the loads in the past were hiding the bottlenecks. Now that we are more balanced, we see the whole process more clearly. In fact, I think that my next challenge is in the Negotiation step. This is step 9 ·in the 10 Steps-of-Sale. My guys spend too much time there and, what's even worse, we give up too much in that phase. I will have to raise that topic in the meeting with my sales management when they all come in. Perhaps I should talk about it with Barry first. By the way, it seems as if nobody remembers the end-of-the-quarter-syndrome. Vanished! Disappeared!

*   *   *

John steps into my office. He mentioned to me the other day that our Cash Machine discussion made him think a lot. He liked the analogy. Perhaps he found some other things that we could learn from it all. He starts the discussion:

"Hi, Roger, there is something I would like to share with you."

"Yes," I ask, curious to know, "I am all ears."

"You know, when you implemented your new incentive scheme, with monthly quotas and the end-of-year buffer and all that stuff, my guys in production really panicked. Especially the managers."

"Why?"

"You know, all our operational systems and measures are geared to quarters. We have a quarterly purchasing plan. We have a quarterly material management cycle. We have a quarterly control system. We produce for quarters. When you moved to a monthly cycle, you almost ignored that we, operationally, are so much quarterly driven. Moving all that operation from quarters to months would have been an enormous task for us. It basically meant that we have to introduce changes, quite significant ones, to all our systems. My guys had all the reasons in the world to panic – big time."

"So why the hell didn't you say anything?"

"Because I thought differently, and now I want to thank you for what you did."

"Thank me?" John succeeds in surprising me. "But why?"

"Roger, you have had a huge positive influence on my operations. You see, my people often do not see the difference between bookings or order taking, and revenues or shipments. When the end-of-the-quarter syndrome kicks in, most bookings come late in the quarter, and if the forecast is wrong, the whole operation becomes a nightmare. Perhaps I should say, not "if" but "when" the forecast is wrong, because this seems to be the case – always."

"So?"

"Your monthly booking cycle has significantly smoothed out the stream of orders during the quarter, so that my quarterly-driven operation can operate in a relatively smooth way, too. A smooth, monthly-driven order stream is a dream when feeding a quarterly driven operation. It is not because we get orders earlier in the quarter that we necessarily need to deliver early in the quarter. We can simply plan better. It appears to be that most of the delivery pressure in our production system is of internal origin. In other words, we rush deliveries to meet revenue targets. Very often, customers can be flexible and even when we get early orders, we can influence the delivery schedule. More than that, it all enables us to reduce WIP inventories, and even to reduce some of the resources that we once needed to deal with the peaks at quarter ends. What else can a guy in production ask for but lower costs and higher efficiencies? I really think that you deserve big hugs from all of us in Production."

"Thanks, John, this really warms my heart. Thanks a lot to you too."

"And let me add one more comment." I ask myself if John will surprise me again. "This is all an issue of visibility, of product mix and of production volume."

"What do you mean, John?"

"When we have low visibility of customer demand, when product mix is high, and when volumes are relatively low – which is the case for CGS – a smooth order entry stream has a huge impact. To tell you the truth, Roger, every company that has our type of visibility, mix and volume should adopt your method at once."

"Thanks, John, I am flattered, but I hope other companies don't figure it out. After all, we want to maintain our competitive advantage, don't we?"

This was a nice end to a productive conversation. I am glad that solving the end-of-the-quarter syndrome has such a strong impact on the whole Cash Machine. By the way, contrary to John, I believe that all companies would benefit from our new approach, not just those with our type of visibility, mix and volume. Decreasing the noise in the orders stream will positively impact every operation, not just our kind. Perhaps the extent of the benefit may differ, but it will be beneficial. I'll talk to John about that on another day and brainstorm with him.

* * *

I am called to Gary's office. The last time this happened in such an official way, it was to make the gambit between Pierce and me. It's only eighteen months now, but it seems like twenty years ago. So much happened since then. The door is closed. I knock on the door and enter Gary's office. I am surprised to see that Ray is there too.

"Sit down, Roger" Gary seems a bit strange. I know that something is happening. I don't know what. After all, sales have gone up quite significantly since I took over. Stopping with the sales of the Lilly and focusing on turning it into a real product turned out to be the right thing to do. We re-launched it 6 months ago and since then, sales have jumped. Overall, we are now closer to the billion-dollar target than we have ever been. Although we have not focused on that per se, competition is now lagging behind us. Yet, perhaps Ray and Gary hoped for more. Who knows what's going on in their minds? Especially in Ray's.

"Ray had a long discussion with Barry last week on, what did he call it?"

"The Cash Machine," Ray is fast to respond.

"Yes, thanks Ray, the Cash Machine. What a strange way to describe a company that we've taken years to build and develop. At first, we wanted to ask you to tell us what our next bottleneck was, an internal one or an external one. But, Ray and I thought that it would be much simpler to simply let you manage it." I don't know what to say. What exactly do they want from me? "Roger, don't look so surprised. You know that I will retire in six months or so. We want you to take the lead and become the President & CEO of Carmen Graphic Solutions."

"Wow," I think, "I definitely didn't see that coming." I hope they can't tell by my face how I actually feel. But Gary continues in a steady voice: "Until then, as part of the transition, I will step down as President and you will be nominated President and COO. I will focus on Engineering and Production. You will take care of the rest – all components of the Cash Machine. We want you to take full responsibility for that machine. With your help, we will cross the one billion dollar sales mark this year, we're confident about this now. This will be the right time for me to retire and the right time for you to take over."

"Gary, Ray, I don't know what to say. I am flattered. Even more, I am happy. I am thankful for the trust and for the opportunity."

"Roger, frankly, you deserve it." Ray is nicer than I have ever seen him. What a metamorphosis. "I must say that I was very skeptical when Gary came up with the idea of appointing you to the VP Sales position. Today, I must admit it: Gary was right. Now, we want to generate even more cash. Why not? You have the full understanding of how to do it. You'll know where and when to invest. We want you to start as soon as possible."

"As I said, I am flattered and I am honored to take this challenge on. May I ask a question?"

"Ask."

"What about Pierce?"

"Now that you're in charge of the Cash Machine, we assume that you will maximize the potential from the market very soon. We need a new set of qualified prospects, or, how do you call it now, more 'raw material.' We have asked Pierce to focus on business development. With the type of Cash Machine we are developing thanks to you, we could become unbeatable in other synergetic business areas too."

"This is good news. Pierce is a good business closer and has excellent relationships with customers and partners. He'll do a good job."

"Ray and Gary, since we're already here, I want to appoint Eric as VP of Sales. He had done a great job as Northwest Regional Manager. I know his kids live in Oregon, but I'm almost certain he'll be willing to move."

"You have my blessing. It's a good move."

"You have mine, too, Roger."

"Thanks, this is great. I am excited about all this."

"We're already thinking about the second billion, Roger. You know, this never ends."

"I know!"

Annex

1. Purpose

The book that you have just finished reading deals with 3 main business concepts:

1. There is a systematic way to manage the sales operation. Most sales managers are very familiar with all one-on-one sales concepts. However, a sales operation that consists of the simultaneous handling of hundreds, or sometimes even thousands, of opportunities is a whole different story! Nevertheless, there is a systematic way to manage a continuous improvement process in sales operation. More on that later in this annex.

2. The prospect-to-cash chain or funnel in an organization is a tightly linked. The departmental boundaries are usually quite arbitrary. Mismanagement of constraints in such a chain will have an impact on the cash generation of the business. This leads to a business philosophy that we recommend all senior management to adopt and act accordingly. A systematic way to manage the prospect-to-cash operation is simply to apply a wider scope of the sales operation or 'prospect-to-order' chain. In this annex, we will focus on the 'prospect-to-order' operation.

3. The end-of-the-quarter syndrome is not axiomatic! Management can take steps that can significantly diminish, or even overcome the syndrome. The effect such move can have on the business and operational cycles in an organization is huge. This book proposes one solution, but there may be others. We believe that this book offers sufficient details to enable executives' its partial or full implementation.

The purpose of this Annex is to provide a more detailed set of tools to implement the sales operation model proposed in this book.

2. Sales Operation Management

2.1 Reports

All Sales Managers are familiar with some sales management tool. The most basic one is *Microsoft Excel*. More dedicated solutions can be as simple as ACT!, or more comprehensive sales management tools such as the *Siebel* or *Oracle* applications. The latter ones are meant to be part of the wide CRM (Customer Relationship Management) systems that are now implemented on a wide scale. Whatever the system or the tool, the following information is typically recorded, for each and every opportunity:

- Name of the Sales Person

- Name of territory

- Name of the customer

- Name or type of opportunity (typically a free description of the configuration in question)

- Sales Stage (or step-of-sale)

- List of products

- Price of deal in this opportunity

- Estimated closure date

- Percentage of probability of closure on or before estimated closure date

- Binary probability of closure on or before estimated closure date

Different Sales Managers will a have different approaches. Some will rely more on a binary probability (the deal will or will not close on time as per my judgment), while some prefer the totals of the percentage probabilities. Some split the percentage probability to 'probability-of-buying' (from any supplier) and to the 'probability-of-buying-from-us' (in case a purchase happens). Various acronyms are used for those terms. This leads to various follow up methods on competition and market share.

2.2 Sales Stages

What follows now is a reminder of the 10 steps of sales (also referred to in some places as 'sales stages'). Many businesses define sales stages in a different way than the one defined in this book (in most cases, one refers to 4 to 6 stages). Our recommendation is to gradually increase the number of defined sales stages to a number close to 10. This will improve the control over the sales operation as well as the ability to manage the continuous improvement process. When an opportunity reaches a certain sales stage, the opportunity is in anticipation for the completion of that specific sales stage. For example, a sales opportunity that is in stage 'production demo' is an opportunity in which all previous stages have been completed, and is now expecting the completion of the 'production demo stage.' Similarly, a sales opportunity that is at the 'negotiation' stage is the sales opportunity in which not all the terms have been concluded and the completion of the negotiation is pending. The table below summarizes the sales stages and mentions what can trigger the completion of that specific stage and hence the move to the next sales stage.

In anticipation for the completion of:	Completion of that stage defined by:
1. Selection	Prospect is entered in a list of customers to call. Prospect is defined as lead.
2. Qualification	Prospect has explicitly expressed need for a solution.
3. Needs assessment	All questions were submitted to prospect and sufficient answers were obtained to understand the prospect's needs in order to move to the next step.
4. Letter of Understanding	A letter of understanding was sent to the prospect.

5. Presentation demo	The product was presented to the prospect in general terms (not yet with the prospect's own data or jobs).

6. Solution Proposal and Technical Check	A technical solution was internally suggested. That solution will be the one demonstrated and then put in the quotation.
7. Production demo	A demo with a job submitted by the prospect was performed and completed.
8. Quotation submission	First quotation was sent to customer, We refer here to a quotation that is the basis for the negotiation process and not to the pro-forma quotations that are sometimes sent to customers for their own processes (budgeting process, purchase requisition process, etc.)
9. Negotiation	Prospect has shaken hands to express agreement, or prospect has signed on last quotation submitted.
10. Closing	Prospect has submitted a formal purchase order.

A typical and simplified report for a specific quarter and for a single Sales Manager with 4 sales persons may look as follows:

The Cash Machine

Sales Person	Customer	Price of Deal [K$]	Sales Stage	Binary Probability	Binary '1' Opportunities
John	A	500	Win	1	500
John	B	450	Negotiation	1	450
John	C	2,000	Closing	1	2,000
John	D	200	Quotation submission	1	200
John	E	25	Negotiation	1	25
John	F	350	Win	1	350
Laura	G	240	Closing	1	240
Laura	H	100	Letter of Understanding	0	0
Laura	I	300	Negotiation	0	0
Laura	J	400	Letter of Understanding	0	0
Laura	K	800	Negotiation	0	0
Laura	L	50	Negotiation	1	50
Laura	M	2,500	Quotation submission	0	0
Eric	N	300	Needs assessment	1	300
Eric	O	260	Technical Check	0	0
Eric	P	240	Letter of Understanding	0	0
Eric	Q	150	Presentation demo	0	0
Eric	R	270	Quotation submission	1	270
Eric	S	820	Production demo	1	820
Eric	T	340	Negotiation	1	340
Sean	U	450	Presentation demo	1	450
Sean	W	500	Closing	1	500
Sean	X	230	Closing	1	230
Sean	Y	450	Production demo	0	0
Sean	Z	1,000	Presentation demo	1	1,000
Sean	AA	200	Technical Check	1	200
Sean	BB	250	Closing	1	250
Sean	CC	600	Win	1	600
Sean	DD	740	Win	1	740
Sean	EE	150	Quotation submission	0	0
Total Opportunities:		*14,865*	*Total Binary '1' Opportunities:*		*9,515*

This is indeed the data that most Sales Managers will work with. Sales Managers will be familiar with each and every case. The sales stage definitely gives an indication of how far away we are from process closure. The total for all opportunities is close to 15M$. The total for binary '1' opportunities is below 10M$. Some of the orders were received already (those are the 'win' cases). Although it may be okay for ongoing management of sales activities, it's not sufficient to drive the continuous improvement process. It doesn't point to where my weakest link is.

Instead, we propose two sets of reports:

1. At any point in time a report of all dollar opportunities per sales stage. This is the **Funnel Report**. It is recommended that this snapshot be measured at the middle and end of each quarter. This report should take into account all the ongoing sales opportunities. Neither the binary nor the percentage probability should interfere here. Also, the estimated time of closure should not be taken into account. In short, all opportunities need to appear in that report. At first, we recommend taking only sales stage 3 (needs assessment) and above for that report. This report will also provide a comparison to the theoretical capacity of the sales force for each sales stage at a certain period of time.

2. For the second report, the same data as above can be used, plus one additional set of data: how long does each and every sales stage take. This report needs to take all opportunities that were closed (win or loss) from a certain point in time in the past (minimum of one full quarter). This report is called the **Constraint Report.**

2.3 An example of Implementation

A simple way to describe and explain the possible outcome of such reports is to use the rule of three. In other words, let's assume a sales force of three sales persons. Each sales person has three opportunities and each opportunity has three sales stages. The three sales persons are A, B, and C. Each one of them works on three opportunities: A1, A2, A3, B1, B2, B3, C1, C2 and C3. The three sales stages are I, II and III. We will call this company '**Simplistic.**'

Simplistic started operations in January with a basket of opportunities of $4 million. All sales cycles started on January 1st. **Simplistic**'s executive management holds its mid-year review meeting. It is mid-July. Most management members remember the traditional sales report at the end of Q1, as follows:

The Cash Machine

Sales Person	Customer	Price of Deal [K$]	Sales Stage	Binary Probability	Binary '1' Opportunities
A	A1	350	Sales Stage III	1	350
A	A2	540	Sales Stage II	1	540
A	A3	100	Win	1	100
B	B1	600	Sales Stage II	1	600
B	B2	510	Sales Stage III	1	510
B	B3	450	Win	1	450
C	C1	200	Sales Stage III	1	200
C	C2	350	Sales Stage II	1	350
C	C3	900	Sales Stage II	1	900

At the mid-Q2 sales review, the obvious conclusions were drawn and everybody worked on moving all sales cycles in the right direction. The above report is an excellent tracking report. It helps to manage and monitor the ongoing sales activities.

Now, for the mid-year review, *Simplistic*'s management does not want to talk on each opportunity and see how it can progress. *Simplistic*'s management wishes to significantly improve its sales operation. In other words, make it more efficient. The dry data that follows is the basis for further reports:

Sales Person	Opportunity	Deal Amount in K$	Moved to Sales Stage I on:	Moved to Sales Stage II on:	Moved to Sales Stage III on:	Won the deal on:
A	A1	350	1-Jan	15-Jan	15-Mar	15-Apr
A	A2	540	1-Jan	10-Jan	3-May	4-Jul
A	A3	100	1-Jan	25-Jan	25-Feb	25-Mar
B	B1	600	1-Jan	31-Jan	3-Apr	25-Apr
B	B2	510	1-Jan	1-Feb	2-Mar	4-May
B	B3	450	1-Jan	12-Jan	31-Jan	20-Feb
C	C1	200	1-Jan	25-Jan	13-Mar	5-Jun
C	C2	350	1-Jan	15-Feb	3-Jun	24-Jun
C	C3	900	1-Jan	5-Jan	1-Apr	1-May

As we can see, *Simplistic*'s sales force of three won all opportunities. Let's now look at the following data from the ***Constraint Report***:

Sales Person	Opportunity	Deal Amount in K$	Days Spent on Sales Stage I:	Days Spent on Sales Stage II:	Days Spent on Sales Stage III:
A	A1	350	14	60	30
A	A2	540	9	113	61
A	A3	100	24	30	30
B	B1	600	30	63	22
B	B2	510	30	31	62
B	B3	450	11	19	20
C	C1	200	24	48	82
C	C2	350	44	108	21
C	C3	900	4	86	30
Average # of days spent per Sales Stage:			*21*	*62*	*40*

The **Constraint Report** presents clearly that **Sales Stage II** takes the most time. For opportunity **A2**, it even took 113 days to complete that stage.

Let's now have a look at the **Funnel Report**, as of March 30, the end of Q1.

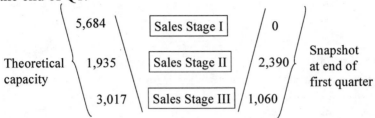

On March 30, there were K$2,390 worth of opportunities in Sales Stage II and were K$1,060 worth of opportunities in Sales Stage III. Assuming that all the sales force would only work on Sales Stage II for a full quarter, and knowing that the average length of Sales Stage II is 62 days and the average opportunity is K$444, the theoretical quarterly capacity of Sale Stage II is K$1,935.

The main conclusion is that Sales Stage II is a constraint. There are more opportunities in that sales stage in a certain quarter than can theoretically be dealt with. **Simplistic**'s management knows where to focus: Sales Stage II!

3. Summary

The traditional sales report of opportunities helps to manage the ongoing sales activities. However, it leaves the continuous improvement process of the sales operation to the intuition of the Sales Manager. We offer a systematic improvement process for better results.

The **Constraint Report** helps to analyze where the constraint of the sales process is. The **Constraint Report** ignores the dollar amount associated with each and every opportunity. The *Funnel Report* provides a good indication on the ratios between the different stages. In a balanced funnel, earlier sales stages should have a higher dollar value than later stages. The ratios vary from company to company, and depend on the market behavior and on competition. When later stages start to have more value than earlier stages, it means that the funnel does not receive a sufficient inflow of new opportunities. Lastly, the *Funnel Report* also provides an indication of actual status per stage *versus* theoretical capacity. This is another indication for the identification of a constraint in the sales process.

GOAL
120% buffer

+20 x 66% = 14   +20 x 33½ = 7

GREEN   120% Payout ·114
·10°

YE ~~TARGET~~ 100 expected growth
TARGET   3 expected growth
95% = PY? — — — — — — —
90% TARGET

DOLLARS
- could be
Gross $
or
Calc'd
profit
#(acting
as buffer)
to limit
Complex Sales

100/12 120% Grow 114³% Yellow 110% Payout
107 RED
10'
expected target or growth for year

could make
the 100%
expected
sales
goal
for ?
which
+X %
140%?

Complex
goals → Specific tactical efforts to be shown in T/a No. t complexing
incentive gives   1 #

• Pay each month as you go along that ①#

YTP
JAN - GRN - Pay   is in green YTD @ 50% (escrow) @ midyear
Feb - Yell - No   You could go to 75% YTD payout s by month
MAR - GRN - Pay   Since your trend is more solid Eliminates QTR RUNS
+ makes
up Feb
GAP •   District RY6 charts would have dots
identified by Rep Name and size of dot based
on % of District Goal
IE, District Goal 100
Rep 1 = 10 = o
Rep 2 = 15 = o
Rep 3 = 20 = ○

• Rep Graph shows ~~trend~~ actual path from month
to month

• Region chart Show Districts same as Reps
w/in Districts and have individual
district charts that show actual path

• Green = Above tgt, clear the road for them use on other
• Yellow = on tgt for expected growth, define habit + grow
• RED = at Risk or below std, eliminate outside task, define pla